rape:
the price of coercive sexuality

rape:
the price of coercive sexuality

Lorenne M.G. Clark
& Debra J. Lewis

the women's press
toronto, canada

Canadian Cataloguing in Publication Data

Clark, Lorenne M.G.
    Rape

Bibliography: p.
ISBN 0-88961-033-X bd.   ISBN 0-88961-032-0 pa.

1. Rape—Canada.   2. Rape. I. Lewis, Debra J.
II.Title.

HV6569.C2C53   364.1'53   C77-001544-1

Cover design by Vita Churchill
Typeset at Women's Educational Press in co-operation with The Coach House Press,
    Toronto, Ontario, Canada

Printed and bound at The John Deyell Company, Willowdale, Ontario, Canada
Lithographed by union labour at The John Deyell Company, Lindsay, Ontario, Canada

Published by Women's Educational Press, Toronto, Ontario, Canada

To Barbara, the two Andreas, Caroline, Diane, Pat, Pam, Carol, Liz, Lynda, Susan, Sharon, and all the other terrific women who made the Toronto Rape Crisis Centre a reality.

contents

part 2   *analysis and critique*

tables

acknowledgments

Thanks are due to many people for helping to make possible the study from which this book developed. First, thanks go to all the women who helped to organize, and continue to operate, the Toronto Rape Crisis Centre. It was out of our involvement with these women that we began to see the full implications of rape in contemporary Canadian society. A large share of the thanks must also go to the Metropolitan Toronto Police Department, which allowed us access to material in their files. The Centre of Criminology, University of Toronto, helped to ease us through the financially-thin first phase of the project and sustained us with moral support throughout. Part of the original research was supported by a small grant from the Humanities and Social Sciences Research Fund, administered through the University of Toronto.

While this book does not deal directly with our further research, we would like to take this opportunity to thank the National Law Reform Commission for funding the court phases of this work. Professor Hans Mohr, who understood the importance of the research, has been a major support as well as a good friend. We are also grateful to the Donner Foundation for funding a comparative study in Western Canada. As soon as it was apparent how little rape research had been done in Canada, and how important it was to develop a national picture of the offence, both the National Law Reform Commission and the Donner Foundation were quick to assist us.

We would also like to thank Ms. Susan Peterson, who was involved in the early stages of the research and produced a paper entitled "Rape and the Male Protection Racket"; this was primary bibliographical research done as background to the project, and in fulfillment of an outside minor in Criminology.

preface

When we first decided to write a book about rape in Canada, we were acutely conscious that it would be the first Canadian book on the subject and, of course, we wanted it to do absolutely everything. We wanted to make Canadian women totally conscious of every aspect of the problem. We wanted to appeal to everyone—those with a great deal of knowledge about the criminal justice system, those with a thorough academic training in the social sciences, and those who knew nothing of any of these matters. Thus, the first draft of the book suffered from what we felt was a decidedly bifurcated vision. We were attempting to deal with two completely different audiences and, in a sense, with two separate problems. Most women want to know about rape because they want to know how to cope with it, if it should ever happen to them. All women need this information, regardless of their other interests or professional commitments. But we also wanted to present the actual data surrounding the offence, the victim, and the offender as it emerged from our empirical study, in a way which would be acceptable to those in the social science disciplines. Our desire to do a first-class job of presenting the study was motivated primarily by the desire to rest our theoretical approach to rape on an absolutely solid and unassailable basis of empirical fact.

In reworking the manuscript, we felt that the most satisfactory way to accomplish our major objectives of getting the actual facts before the public, and of presenting a developed theory of rape which could account for these facts, was to begin by presenting the data emerging from the study, within only a very general feminist perspective. This was the frame of reference with which we first began the project, and it was unabashedly our perspective on this and every other issue with which we were concerned both as women and as "professionals". We felt that all women, regardless of background, education, or work orientation, would be familiar with at least some recent feminist writing on rape, and would therefore be able to approach the results of the study from a common framework.

The data emerging from the study does not itself rest on any particular view of rape, either feminist or non-feminist. Nevertheless, we feel that the specific theoretical model which we develop in chapters 7 through 12 is the best model to use in *interpreting* the data and its meaning. The feminist perspective we sketch in chapter 1 is meant to provide only a general account of recent approaches to the problem of rape, and to describe the framework within which we ourselves approached our work. But it is not assumed in the presentation of the data, and some aspects of it later come under criticism when we develop our own specific theory. The data from the study stands on its own two (or perhaps four) feet, and it was for this reason that we presented it outside a specific framework of analysis. No matter what the background of the individual reader, the data can be assessed independently of the authors' perspective.

However, as theoreticians and committed feminists, we also felt a strong responsibility to develop a comprehensive theory of the historical role of women, and to show the specific role played by the evolution of the offence of rape. This theory is the framework of analysis which explains the facts and outlines solutions to the problems delineated. Though chapters 2 through 6 can be read independently of everything else in the book, we feel that the full impact of the facts can be assessed only within an adequate framework of analysis, and that the validity of our theory is much more convincing in the light of the facts presented.

What should be done about rape is a question which cannot be debated without facts, but it cannot be decided without theory either. As we make clear throughout the book, change— in particular, legal and procedural change—is one of our major objectives. And our reasons for thinking that these changes are important are firmly embedded within our theoretical perspective. It is our fundamental belief that the problems of women in contemporary Canadian society do not come from simple malfunctions in our social and legal system, and cannot therefore be solved by simple solutions. Radical change is needed, and in our view, radical change is structural change. But even for those who may reject that view, we hope that our book goes some way towards showing that this is at least a plausible position, and that our theory provides a comprehensive, analytic framework with which to assess other proposed solutions which may be offered to various aspects of the problem of rape.

part 1
the phenomenon
of rape

1
the problem of rape

The fear of rape affects all women. It inhibits their actions and limits their freedom, influencing the way they dress, the hours they keep, and the routes they walk. The fear is well founded, because no woman is immune from rape.

But in the public mind there are two quite different attitudes to rape, the rape victim, and the rape offender. At times we condemn rape as a monstrous, criminal act; at others, we slough it off as a mildly dirty joke, treating it as nothing more serious than a minor skirmish in the inevitable "battle of the sexes".

As the archetypal, antisocial crime, rape is kept alive in the public conscience by sensational newspaper accounts of grisly sex-murders, presented as titillating warnings to young women about the dangers of hitch-hiking or other "unladylike" conduct. This reinforces what every woman has been taught from childhood —rape is the worst thing that can happen to a woman. Within this perspective, rape calls forth our greatest moral outrage and our greatest cry for vengeance. But co-existing with these attitudes are others, in which rape is dismissed with a knowing wink as a natural consequence of the sexual game in which man pursues and woman is pursued. What is called "rape", then, is thought to be only an unsophisticated seduction; at most, it is a minor breach of our social standards.

This contradiction in public attitudes is reflected in society's inconsistent treatment of rapists and rape victims. At the level of codified law and public pronouncements, we repudiate rape as a serious offence. Our laws against rape imply that the accepted moral standard of sexual relations is one of mutual consent, where neither party uses any kind of physical coercion or threat. But at the level of actual practice, women have found little real protection in the judicial system. Few cases come to court, fewer rapists are convicted, and the victim, rather than the rapist, is put on trial. Our courts do not fulfill the promise of the law, and rape remains a serious threat to women.

Among the many questions to be answered, the most basic ones are "Why are some rape victims taken seriously while others are not?" and "Why are some rapists punished while the overwhelming majority are not?" It is clear that we lack an analysis which can explain both the myths and the realities of rape. And it is also clear that, without a deeper understanding of what rape is and why it occurs, we can never eliminate the problems surrounding it, much less eliminate rape itself.

We believe that the most compelling insights into rape were first achieved by the women's movement. While it is impossible and unimportant to date very precisely the point at which popular articles dealing with rape first began to appear, it is evident that they were a direct result of the women's movement developing in the late 1960s, that they first appeared in feminist publications, and that they were written by avowed feminists. For all practical purposes, the popular reaction to the problem of rape began with an article by Susan Griffin in *Ramparts Magazine* in 1971.[1] This article, entitled "Rape: The All-American Crime", was a powerful attack on some basic assumptions which seemed to dominate official attitudes towards rape and rape victims. Her tone was strident, and her first concern was to set before the reading public the feelings and reactions of women. Nowhere in the rape literature was there any record of how women, the victims of rape, felt about the offence, either in terms of their own personal experience of rape, or in terms of the judgments made about them by others. While many people in the academic community were aware of the risks run by a rape victim in reporting the offence, no one had thought it significant to document, or even explore, the truth of the feminists' allegation that the trial of a rape offender was also—perhaps primarily—the trial of a rape victim. This view of the rape victim as the victim not only of a criminal act but of the judicial process as well, continues to dominate much recent writing on the subject.

During the early 1970s, rape relief or crisis centres sprang up across North America with the dual purpose of providing support to rape victims, and pressuring governmental and other public agencies for changes which would lessen the impact on the victim of reporting the offence. Independent groups and persons—"independent" in the sense that they had no connections with official institutions or with the academic, social scientific community—began to carry out detailed studies; they examined both the methods used by the police, the courts, and the medical profession in dealing with rape victims, and attitudes which members of these institutions brought with them to their tasks. These investigators had an admitted and partial objective: they wished to document the more general thesis that rape was just another form of women's oppression in a sexist society which assumed the natural inequality of the sexes, and the natural domination and superiority of the male.

They called attention to the fact that rape was not treated as a serious offence, despite the heavy maximum sentences allowed by law, and to the common belief that most women who were raped simply got what they were asking for or deserved. They substantiated their claims by pointing to alarming increases in rape's rate of occurrence, despite rape victims' continuing reluctance to report the offence, low ratios of "founded" to "unfounded" cases at the level of police classification, the special rules of evidence used to discredit rape victims in court, low conviction rates, and sentences far, far below the maximums. If a belief in the moral gravity of the offence existed in the public consciousness, it did not filter down to the only levels upon which it could be acted. As these writers concluded, with justification, the divergence between alleged values about rape and the actual practices surrounding it constituted but another, glaring instance of the hypocrisy of a male supremacist society. While the laws against rape were supposed to represent real respect for the sanctity and purity of womanhood, their implementation reflected the true value placed upon women in our society.

Another fact which feminist writers hammered home again and again was the virtual conspiracy of silence surrounding the whole question of rape. As a very grave and outrageous act, it is assumed to be an unusual occurrence, and this assumption is thought to justify the fact that rape isn't much talked about. In fact, rape happens a great deal, and is happening with greater frequency everywhere. But like incest and wife-beating, it was for a very long time one of those embarrassing facets of the human condition that one simply did not mention. This silence no doubt reflects the common belief that rape doesn't happen very often, but it also reflects the opinion that even if rape does occur, it should not, and therefore it shouldn't be made public. As far as the victim is concerned, the prevailing attitude is that rape is shameful and degrading to *her*, and the less said about it the better. Advertising the fact that one has been raped is an open invitation to social disaster.

Even the courts have adopted the attitude that public knowledge of rape trials should be kept to a virtual minimum. To publicize the increase in rape is to bring shame on one's community, and may even operate, some claim, to cause an even greater increase in the rate of occurrence. The correct policy is silence; some forms of human behaviour are inevitable, but they should not be dignified with public attention. This attitude has prevailed with respect to research as well. The less we know about the more shameful acts of human beings, the better off we are, or so it is implied.

From any perspective, this represents a decidedly ostrich-like stance. We cannot help what we do not know about. But the general assumption seems to be that more knowledge about rape would not allow us to do anything about it, since we are powerless to prevent it, and we may as well insulate ourselves from its reality as best we can. This is a view which accepts rape as an inevitable accompaniment of human society, a *natural* fact that we must learn to live with.

The net effect of this conspiracy of silence is to discourage many rape victims from reporting the offence. Silence perpetuates the misconception that rape does not happen very often (who wants to look like the rare case of disaster?); it reinforces the view of rape as a shameful and degrading experience (who wants to reveal herself as having suffered a woman's worst fate?); and it reflects the belief that "nice girls don't get raped" (who wants to advertise that she's been raped, given the automatic implication that she wasn't then, and certainly isn't now, a "nice girl"?). To the extent that our society's silence rests on a presumption that rape is a natural fact, and that there can, hence, be no point in prosecuting rape offenders beyond a simple desire for revenge, the women who report rape appear to be tilting at windmills for no better purpose than revenging an affront to their outraged dignity. If rape is seen as a natural (though regrettable) event, a source of shame to its victim, and a crime of low incidence which mainly affects women who in some sense invited it, what woman in her right mind would want to avail herself of the slim chance of justice afforded by the judicial process, particularly when her motivation is likely to be perceived purely as a desire for vengeance?

The conclusion which the feminist writers reached was that social attitudes and the legal and judicial processes all conspire to keep women from having effective exercise of their political and human rights. Despite the fact that laws against rape exist on the books, ostensibly for women's protection, there are effective social and legal constraints which prevent women from utilizing their legal rights. The law is the illusory pot of gold at the end of an illusory rainbow, according women neither the protection of their rights nor the guarantee of redress for their injuries. Women are afraid, and are made afraid, to seek the protection and redress of the law. Their best strategy is to remain silent, and when one considers that it is the rapist who has most to benefit from this silence, it is hard to escape the conclusion that social attitudes, and their articulation in the legal process, operate to protect not the victim but the rapist. As things stand, it is *being* raped that is punished, and it is being raped that is the crime.

It has been argued that rape is simply the ultimate weapon which men use to exercise power over women and to exhibit that alleged natural domination which is their assumed birthright.[2] Many feminists contend that rape is as much an expression of the need to illustrate that power, as it is an expression of the desire for sexual gratification, and that the exercise of that power is condoned and encouraged by existing attitudes and practices. If the laws against rape provided the model of consensual sexuality which some assume they do, serving as much as an ideal to be striven for, as an articulation of the basic standards to be maintained, and if these laws were enforced with that goal in mind, then the inequality of power between the sexes upon which male supremacy rests would disappear. But those in control of our society do not want that imbalance of power to disappear; therefore, they have a vested interest in undermining the extent to which the laws against rape could constitute such an ideal. In order to preserve and enhance male supremacy, rape must be both possible and probable; it must remind women who has power over them and keep them solidly in their places. Thus, it is hardly surprising that the practices surrounding rape are what they are; to preserve the sexual *status quo*, it is not accidental, but *necessary*, that they remain so.

One of the most important contributions which the feminists made was to force people to see rape in a larger social, economic and political perspective. The social scientists who tried to deal "objectively" with the problem of rape never seemed aware that rape takes place within a social setting, and that it cannot be treated or analyzed apart from the larger framework of social attitudes and practices in which it is embedded. This led them to make many assumptions which were clearly false, and a good many more which were highly questionable. Most importantly, the social scientists never really asked why rape occurs, and what social attitudes and beliefs support it. They brought their own biases with them into their research but conducted their research, and drew their conclusions, as if those biases did not exist. Whatever claims may have been made about the "objectivity" of the social sciences, even a cursory study of the rape literature reveals much to contradict it.

One of our basic contentions is that rape is a *social*, not a natural fact. It is produced by a certain kind of society and not by an eternal, immutable human nature. The attempt to treat rape as a natural fact, as an inevitable consequence of a fixed human nature, is simply a way to avoid doing anything important about it. But if rape is a social fact, it can be eliminated through social change.

Some people may believe that certain social arrangements are necessitated by some fixed aspects of human nature, and they may or may not believe that rape can be eliminated, depending on what aspects of human nature they take to be constant, and what social arrangements they take to be not merely conventional, but necessary because of it. If rape is really believed to be a problem, however, expediency surely dictates that we at least try to rearrange society and to change the natures adapted to suit the present one, in an attempt to eliminate not merely the adverse consequences of the problem, but the cause and the problem itself. It is our deeply-held conviction that the causes of rape lie within the present social system, a system which is, among other things, fundamentally sexist. Rape is one of the products of a sexist society; it is the price we must pay for a society based on coercive sexuality.

It was from the feminist perspective outlined above, that we began the project on which this book is based. Both of us had been deeply involved with the women's movement in Canada: Lorenne had first been concerned with the issue of day care, and then with abortion; Debra had had a long involvement with birth control counselling and abortion referral. Following a year and a half at law school, Lorenne had begun teaching a graduate course on the morality of the Canadian criminal justice system at the Centre of Criminology, University of Toronto, and Debra had enrolled in the Centre of Criminology's M.A. programme. We were both aware that rape was a problem with which other women had been deeply concerned, and together with about twenty other women, we had just begun to organize the Toronto Rape Crisis Centre, which opened on February 14, 1974. But the process of organizing the crisis centre made us all quickly aware that no one knew what dimensions the problem of rape had assumed in Canada. There was a dearth of literature on the subject. At that time, only one small empirical study, originating from the Clarke Institute of Psychiatry under the direction of Professor J.W. Mohr,[3] had been carried out. Neither we nor anyone else really knew what the facts were with respect to the incidence, rate of reporting, police attitudes towards rape and rape victims, medical approaches, conviction rates, trial procedures, or the ultimate disposition and treatment of offenders. All of the issues that had been raised and/or documented in the United States, had not been investigated in Canada at all.

We decided that a preliminary study which would at least give us an opening into the problem could be handled as the subject of Debra's M.A. Thesis, under Lorenne's supervision.[4] We thought that a good place to start would be at the point where a rape victim first comes into contact with the criminal justice system, in the form of the police. One of the main criticisms raised by feminists elsewhere had been that the police handling of rape and rape victims was prejudiced, highly selective, and often worse than the rape itself. We wanted to assess whether or not what was true elsewhere was also true in Canada, or at least in Metropolitan Toronto.

With these thoughts in mind, and fully aware of the problems we were likely to face in attempting to investigate these aspects of the problem, we set about drafting our research proposal. At the time, we were totally unaware of just how great a problem rape is, not only as a phenomenon experienced daily by women, but as a microcosm of what passes for "normal" sexual relations between men and women. No other subject better illustrates the terrible price women pay for living in a fundamentally sexist society, and it is not accidental that the issues which most deeply concern feminists have all revolved around the female sexual and reproductive function. The logical end of such concerns is an analysis of rape.

Part 1 of this book presents the results of our empirical study, which is described in the next chapter. It also gives a picture of the process which a rape victim goes through after she reports the offence to the police, and examines the particular kind of rape case that leads to successful prosecution. Part 2 discusses the findings of Part 1, provides an analytic framework with which to assess the data, and criticizes current academic theories of rape.

2
research project: description and methodology

Early in the fall of 1973 we presented our proposal to the Metropolitan Toronto Police Department, requesting access to all cases of rape reported to them during the year 1970 and permission to interview the reporting complainants. We chose 1970 as our "target" year in order to ensure that none of the cases studied would still be involved in the legal process. From the beginning, we saw the project only as the first stage of a larger study.[1] The Police Department readily granted our first request, but would not allow us to interview reporting rape victims. Their denial was based on a consideration of the problems of confidentiality. They were extremely concerned to keep the victims, the defendants, and all information about them, confidential, and felt that allowing us to interview victims would seriously prejudice their confidential relations with the complainants. Because of the same considerations, they also removed, by blacking out, the names of all complainants, defendants, and material witnesses from the reports they made available to us. We were provided with xeroxed copies of the General Occurrence Reports, which are the standard forms filled out by police officers for each reported offence. (See Appendix A.) We were required to work on these forms in the offices of the central Police Department, and made up our own data sheet, designed to utilize all the available material. (See Appendix B.)

We considered only those cases defined as "rape" under Section 143 of the Criminal Code, which reads as follows:

> RAPE
> 143. A Male person commits rape when he has sexual intercourse with a female person who is not his wife,
>> (a) without her consent, or
>> (b) with her consent if the consent
>>> (i) is extorted by threats or fear of bodily harm,
>>> (ii) is obtained by personating her husband, or
>>> (iii) is obtained by false and fraudulent representations as to the nature and quality of the act.[2]

The sentencing provisions governing the commission of this offence are covered under Section 144:

> PUNISHMENT FOR RAPE
> 144. Everyone who commits rape is guilty of an indictable offence and is liable to imprisonment for life.[3]

We excluded all cases of "attempted rape" because of the difficulties of distinguishing these from cases classified as "indecent assault". Since including all three categories ("rape", "attempted rape" and "indecent assault") in our data base would have meant including many assault cases in which rape was not the intent of the offender, we decided to restrict the study to those cases where rape was clearly the intent of the offender.

In addition, we decided to exclude those reported rapes in which the victim was under fourteen years of age. Again, there were a number of reasons for this decision. First, rapes in this category may be prosecuted under either Section 143 (quoted above), or under Section 146.[4] Under this section, the consent of the victim is not an issue because a female under fourteen years of age cannot legally consent to intercourse. In addition, we hypothesized that an offender might have different motivations for sexually assaulting a younger, rather than an adult or near-adult woman.

Our immediate research objectives were to determine the following:

1. The number of rapes reported to the Metropolitan Toronto Police Department in 1970, comparing this figure with figures for previous years in order to determine whether reported rape was becoming more frequent.
2. Monthly, weekly and daily patterns for the occurrence of rape.
3. Relevant data on rape victims, including national origin, age, marital status, educational and employment background, and physical appearance.
4. Relevant data on rapists, including national origin, age, marital status, educational and employment backgound, physical description, and any other data which would allow us to build up a psychosocial profile of the rapist.
5. Details of the crime itself, including location, relationship between rapist and victim, the frequency of violence, use or threatened use of a weapon, and frequency of arrest.
6. Factors affecting police classification of reported rapes as "founded" or "unfounded".

Also, we set ourselves the following questions to answer:

1. What is the ratio of founded to unfounded rape reports?
2. Why are false reports made? Are they vindictive?
3. Is there any evidence to suggest that some victims are "participants" in the rape, and that they somehow "invite" what happens to them?
4. How do the rapes themselves differ from one another?
5. How do police perceptions of the rape vary, according to the presence or nature of a relationship between the victim and the rapist?
6. How do police perceptions vary in accordance with other factors, such as the victim's marital status, her socio-economic background, and whether or not she had been drinking at the time of the offence?
7. What, if any, are the particular difficulties of young victims?
8. Who rapes—that is, what are the racial and ethnic backgrounds of offenders, and what are their socio-economic histories?
9. Is there any evidence to suggest that rape is primarily an unpremeditated event triggered by uncontrollable sexual desires?
10. What are the psychodynamics of the rapist?
11. What do public attitudes towards rape, the victim and the rapist imply about the social relationships of men and women?

12. Is rape really treated as a serious crime?

Our data base consisted of 116 reported rapes of women over fourteen years of age. These cases provided data on 117 rape complainants and 129 offenders. There are more complainants than cases because one reported rape involved 2 victims, and there are more offenders than cases because 8 reported rapes involved more than one offender. There were 108 cases of single-offender rape, 6 cases involving 2 offenders, and 2 cases of group rape, involving 3 and 6 offenders respectively. Thus, 7.4% of the reported rapes which we examined involved multiple offenders.

The police classified 42, or 36.2% of these cases as founded. This meant that they would investigate the case further, and lay charges if a suspect was arrested. The remaining 74, or 63.8% of reported rapes were classified as unfounded, and thus terminated.

It is important to note that we dealt with all rapes reported to the police, and not just with those which the police classified as founded. Most previous studies had dealt only with the latter group of cases, and we believed that this procedure was questionable for a number of reasons. One of the things we wanted to find out was whether or not Canadian police departments were prejudiced in dealing with rape cases and rape victims, and it was therefore essential to be able to make an independent judgment on the factors affecting police classification.

An initial perusal of the General Occurrence Reports indicated that police classification of cases as founded was indeed highly selective. Even at this stage, however, it was obvious that police classification was not based on simple bias; it also reflected practical considerations of how successfully cases could be prosecuted if they went to court. All of the cases classified by the police as founded displayed one or more of the following features:

1. The victim was a "credible" witness; that is, she was likely to be believed by a jury because she conformed to established norms of "respectable", "acceptable" female behaviour.
2. The facts of the case were so strong that a founded classification was unavoidable, as when the victim had been badly beaten.
3. The police were in a position to pursue the investigation actively because the victim could name her attacker, or provide information about his whereabouts, place of residence or employment.
4. The police perceived a strong similarity between this particular

case and others currently under investigation.

We agreed that the complainant had been raped in all cases which the police classified as founded.

In examining the cases classified by the police as unfounded we wished to distinguish between cases so classified because no rape had in fact occurred and cases so classified for other reasons. We wished, of course, to see what kinds of "other reasons" were used in order to ascertain the extent to which police treatment of rape victims and classification of reported rape offences were prejudicial. Thus, it was necessary to sort the rape reports deemed by the police to be unfounded into two categories: those which were truly unfounded, that is, cases in which no rape had occurred; and those which were so classified for reasons other than those directly related to whether or not an act of forcible intercourse within the legal definition of "rape" had occurred, and in which there seemed no good reason to disbelieve that the complainant had been raped. The 116 cases in our data base were therefore divided into three categories.

1. *Founded, F.* Those cases classified by the police as founded, which they were prepared to investigate and to pass on to the judicial phases of the criminal justice system if a suspect was arrested. We agreed with the classification of all these cases, and our founded category is the same as that of the police.

2. *Unfounded, U.* Those cases classified by the police as unfounded, where we could find no rational or factual basis for a founded classification. Our own unfounded category was much smaller than that of the police.

3. *Unfounded/Possibly Founded, U/PF.* Those cases classified by the police as unfounded, where it seemed that this classification was not based primarily on an evaluation of whether or not the victim had been raped, but was based on other reasons, and where it appeared to us that there were valid reasons for believing that a rape had, in fact, occurred. We classified cases as unfounded/possibly founded if any of the following conditions were present:

   a. The reason given or implied by the police for an unfounded classification was the unsuitability of the victim as a witness. One such case involved a victim who was found in a distraught state with her clothing disarranged. She complained of pain in her legs, stomach, arms and back. The doctor who examined her found scrapes and bruises on her arms, and confirmed that vaginal penetration had occurred. On the General Occurrence Report, police described this woman in the following way:

> The victim in this case is 26 years of age, she has been separated from her husband since 1963, she has a 4 year old girl...she is on welfare, $150.00 a month...in August of 1969 she was in ——— Hospital, Psychiatric Ward for three weeks...

The picture created here is of a victim who is not likely to make a favourable impression on a jury. However, there was no evidence presented which would suggest that the rape reported by the victim had not in fact occurred.

b. The reason given or implied by the police for an unfounded classification was the lack of solid "corroborative" evidence that would be acceptable in a courtroom. The special rules of evidence which discriminate against rape victims will be discussed in detail in the next chapter, but until 1976, Section 142 of the Criminal Code required the presiding judge at a rape trial to instruct the jury that it was not safe to find the accused guilty in the absence of material evidence which corroborated the victim's testimony that she had been raped by the accused.[5] The victim's word could not stand alone; if her testimony was not supported by other, material evidence, then the jury was warned that it was unsafe to find the accused guilty merely on the basis of her sworn testimony. Although rape cases are particularly difficult to prosecute, we feel that these practical considerations are irrelevant to the fact of whether or not a rape has been committed, and should not affect police classification of a reported offence.

c. The victim wished to cease investigation of the crime. In these cases, the case was classified as unfounded because the victim had become what is technically termed a "hostile witness". It is not a complainant who lays a charge; any criminal offence is an offence against the Crown, and it is the Crown which prosecutes. Thus, the complainant is merely a witness for the Crown. She may become a hostile witness for many reasons. She may fear reprisals from the rapist and his friends; she may be pressured by relatives who fear the publicity of a rape trial; she may learn what kind of questioning she will be subjected to in court. An initially co-operative witness may become "hostile" after several encounters with the police. One victim requested that the investigation of her case be stopped because repeated visits of uniformed policemen to her suburban home had raised the prurient interest of her neighbours, who were asking her two small children embarrassing questions, and subjecting her and her husband to rather obvious forms of social ostracism. When a rape victim becomes hostile to the prosecution, it is very difficult to achieve a conviction. But, again, this is no reason to classify a rape report as unfounded.

d. There was independent evidence, such as the physical condition of the victim or conditions at the scene of the crime, which indicated that a rape had occurred, but the case had nonetheless been classified as unfounded. This was true in the case described in category "a", above. The victim's scrapes and bruises, her emotional distress, and medical corroboration of penetration, all indicated that she had been raped.

e. The police appeared unwilling, for reasons of personal or other prejudice, to investigate a complaint which was otherwise plausible.

These, then, were the guidelines which we used in reclassifying cases as unfounded/possibly founded. In none of these cases was there any material evidence to suggest that the complainant had not been raped; on the contrary, there was sometimes independent evidence in support of her claim. But in addition, there was usually a clear indication of the real reason behind the unfounded classification given by police. In general, it appeared that this classification had been based either on police perceptions of the victim's character, or on an evaluation of how successfully her case could be prosecuted. We concluded that these cases had been improperly classified as unfounded. Factual evidence to suggest that there had been no rape—which was the only justifiable basis for such a classification—was absent in every case. Our subjective impression was that a rape had probably occurred in all of these cases, but for the purposes of our study we have taken a more conservative position, and have labelled them "unfounded/possibly founded".

Using this method of classification, we found that 42 cases fell into the founded category, 62 fell into the unfounded/possibly founded category, and 12 fell into the unfounded category.

	Police	Clark/Lewis	
Founded	42	42	
Unfounded/Possibly Founded	--	62	>104
Unfounded	74	12	
Total	116	116	

Our reclassification immediately provided answers to some of the questions which had motivated our research. First, it was clear that there is a bias in police classification, and that studying only founded rapes would, therefore, produce misleading results.

Secondly, it was obvious that very few women make false rape reports, though it is commonly believed that most rape charges are false and motivated by a desire for revenge. We carefully analyzed the 12 cases which we believed to be genuinely unfounded, to see if this assumption could be supported by our data. In 5 of these cases, the rape was reported to the police by someone other than the victim—a relative, boyfriend, or hospital official. In a further 2 cases, the complainant reported under pressure from others (a boyfriend and a husband, respectively). We classified 2 cases as unfounded because their circumstances seemed highly improbable for the commission of the crime, and one complainant was a destitute woman who was apparently trying to attract attention and support. In the remaining 2 cases, the complainants reported rape out of anger at what they felt was unjustified abuse. One case involved a prostitute who had been beaten and robbed; the other involved a woman who met a man in a bar and desired sexual contact, but was subsequently treated very roughly. Both women readily admitted that a rape had not occurred, once their anger had abated.

Thus, out of 116 reported rapes, only 12, or 10.3%, were, in our view, genuinely unfounded. Only 7, or 6.0%, were false reports made by the alleged victim herself. At most, only 4 of these reports could have been made out of a desire for revenge—those 2 cases which simply did not seem believable in the circumstances, and the 2 which arose out of anger at having been physically abused. And only the first 2 posed any threat to an innocent man, since the complainants in the other 2 cases admitted early in the investigation that no rape had occurred.

However, before presenting the detailed results of the study, some mention must be made of the methodological problems we encountered and of the limitations imposed by the nature of our data source.

The major problem is the limited number of cases available for examination. Clearly, there is a danger involved in drawing conclusions on the basis of a small number of cases. Indeed, there are often problems involved in drawing conclusions on the basis of a large number of cases. In order to make valid generalizations one must be sure, and be able to prove, that the sample of cases analyzed is *representative* of the phenomena under investigation and large enough to illustrate variation within the representative group. Thus, the representativeness, and the size of the sample, are the two major factors which must be assessed in order to estimate the reliability of the data itself and of any conclusions based on it.

In order to assess the degree to which our sample is representative of reported rapes, we have compared our results with those of other studies. And we have tried to investigate the extent to which differences can be accounted for by factors other than non-representativeness of our own data. While it is reasonable to expect some similarities in patterns of rape between one urban centre and another, it is also reasonable to expect the patterns to vary because of sociological factors such as ethnic and racial composition. A major methodological problem besetting our study was the fact that no other research of this kind had ever been done in Canada. Thus, we were constrained to compare our results with data from jurisdictions beyond our borders and this is clearly bound to have some significance. And since all such studies are limited by the nature of the original data source, some differences are bound to result from the fact that methods of reporting rape, informal guidelines to police classification, and courtroom practices will also vary, according to differences in community values and the ways in which these are operationalized in police and court procedures and practices.

However, despite these difficulties, we believed that it was not only valid, but necessary, to compare our results with those emerging from other studies, and to assess both the similarities and the differences between the sets of data. We felt that the similarities which emerged would contribute to our general knowledge about rape, and that the differences which emerged would pinpoint the areas needing more thorough investigation. The studies which we used as sources of comparison were Amir's study of forcible rape in Philadelphia,[6] Chappell and Singer's study of rape in New York City,[7] Chappell, Geis, Schafer and Siegel's comparative study of rape in Boston and Los Angeles,[8] Mohr's earlier study of founded rape reports in Metropolitan Toronto,[9] Ringrose's study of reported cases in Edmonton,[10] and McCaldon's study of convicted rapists serving their sentences in Kingston Penitentiary.[11] All but McCaldon's study used police data as their information source.

The nature of the data itself also presented a problem. Chappell and Singer, in their study of rape in New York City, remarked that investigation of police files "tended to take on the characteristics of a salvage operation, rather than an exercise in sophisticated analysis".[12] We experienced the same problem with the Toronto files. General Occurrence Reports varied considerably, even with respect to the basic factual data. We have noted any missing information on each table, and have avoided extrapolation in those cases where data was unavailable.

Variation also existed in the reporting officers' general descriptions of the rape and its investigation. However, there was a significant quantity of this more subjective kind of data, which we found particularly helpful for two reasons. It described the rapist's behaviour during the crime, and revealed police attitudes towards each case.

Finally, it is important to note that many rapes were simply inaccessible to us as investigators. A very large number of rapes do not appear in any statistics. The percentage of rape which goes unreported is generally agreed to be far greater than the average for most other crimes. Hood and Sparks, for example, estimate that the actual number of rapes occurring is from 5 to 10 times greater than the number reported to the police.[13] Without further study of this larger group, we cannot determine whether there are significant differences between reported and unreported rapes, with regard to their victims, their perpetrators, or any of their circumstances. Until the reasons for non-reporting disappear, we must rely on the research carried out by rape crisis centres, at present the only source of information on unreported rapes.[14]

There are also many cases of rape which do not fit the legal definition. These would include acts of forcible intercourse between husband and wife, for example, since according to the law, a man cannot rape his legal wife. But they would also include all of those cases which could fall under Section 143 of the Criminal Code (which we have used as the basic definition of our study), if they were not classified as other offences, such as murder, attempted murder, incest, indecent assault, assault with intent to cause bodily harm, or common assault.[15] It is quite possible that some rape cases which were reported to the Metropolitan Toronto police in 1970 do not appear in our study. This could have happened if the victim had died as a result of the attack, and the case was therefore classified and investigated as a case of homicide, or if the police decided to proceed with it as a case of incest. It is our belief that many rapes are statistically and socially invisible, precisely because they can so easily be classified as something else.

Despite the limitations of our data, however, we believed that the information contained in the police files was the best available to us at the time, and that it deserved investigation. Hopefully, revisions in police reporting techniques will solve some of the problems we met, and we have made recommendations which we feel would be conducive to this end. But the basic problem made clear by our research is that many women are not willing to report the offence. Fundamental changes at all levels must occur in order to change this situation; we cannot hope to have anything like a complete picture of rape until all victims are willing to report the crime.

In the following chapters in Part 1 of this book, we will look at the facts which emerged from our study, as they relate to the offence of rape itself, to the victim and to the offender. We have disregarded the data from all 12 unfounded cases, since they were clearly unreliable. Thus, of the 116 cases which constituted our original data base, only 104 (the F and U/PF cases) are discussed and tabulated.

Because we have drawn two kinds of information from the data, we have adopted a two-part presentation for many of the variables discussed. First, we have used a bar graph to illustrate the way rape complaints in each category were classified by the police. For example, the bar graph for the variable "Location of Offence" (see page 63) contrasts the F and U/PF classifications for each specific category (in this case, each specific location) within the variable. Where a significant difference between the two classifications exists, that variable probably influences police classification of the offence.

Secondly, we have listed the total number of cases (F plus U/PF) in each category, beneath the bars which illustrate police classification of cases that fell into this category. We have also listed the percentage of cases in each category of the entire data base, in order to indicate the over-all distribution of the data. For example, the figures under the bar graph for "Location of Offence" show where, in fact, most reported rapes in our study took place. We have not listed separately the number of F cases and the number of U/PF cases within each category, but these figures can easily be calculated by multiplying the total number of cases in the category by the percentage of cases described as F or U/PF. Of the 19 reported rapes which took place in the victim's residence, for example, 12 (or 63.2% of 19) were classified by the police as founded.

Thus, Part 1 of this book has a dual function. It presents a picture of rape in Metropolitan Toronto in 1970, and also describes the filtering system which allows only some rape cases to come to court. The reasons *why* this filtering system operates as it does will be analyzed in Part 2. However, before beginning to discuss the features of rape as they emerged from our study, we believe it would be useful to outline the legal processes in which a rape victim becomes involved, once she reports the offence.

3
rape and
the judicial system

In Canada, since rape is an offence under the Criminal Code, it is a federal offence. However, the criminal courts are administered by the provinces and there are therefore some procedural differences between one province and another. In this chapter we will be outlining the procedures used in the province of Ontario. The specific police practices which we describe are those of Metropolitan Toronto.

the victim meets the law

Usually the victim herself makes the first contact with the police, either by telephoning or coming into a division station.[1] At this stage, she will be interviewed by a detective or police constable, either in her home or at the station.[2]

As soon as she reports the offence, and possibly before her first interview, the victim will be instructed to have a medical examination. One of the legal elements of the offence of rape is penetration of the victim's vagina by a penis. A sexual assault can be legally classified as rape if and only if some degree of penetration, however slight, has taken place. It is therefore necessary to prove penetration, and the best witness for this purpose is a qualified medical practitioner who is familiar with the forensic tests required by the police and the courts. These tests must be done within twenty-four hours of the offence and before the victim has taken a bath, which can destroy valuable evidence such as semen in the vagina.

Hospitals vary a great deal in their treatment of rape cases and rape victims. While we were unable to investigate very thoroughly which hospitals were the best and which the worst, we certainly gathered enough information to know that this subject deserves further, very thorough study. Most hospitals do not provide qualified gynaecologists for the victim's medical examination, but leave it to intern and resident staff. These persons are frequently inexperienced, and in addition are reluctant to examine rape victims because they know that this will involve them in several court appearances at which they will be required to give testimony. Furthermore, the less experienced staff members are, the less likely they will be to see themselves as performing a task in support of a police investigation, and the more likely they will be to have, and to express, views about whether or not the victim "really was raped". Since the question as to whether or not an act of sexual contact is "rape" is a legal, and not a medical judgment, doctors should at no time be allowed to make such judgments or to communicate them, either to the victim or to the police.

Our initial impression, from talking to rape crisis centre volunteers in Vancouver and Montreal, was that in these cities there seems to be much less difficulty around acquisition of medical evidence, and the impact of the medical examination on rape victims, than there is in Toronto. This difference seems directly traceable to the fact that in both Vancouver and Montreal, all rape victims are examined by a doctor appointed by the police department, who is thoroughly familiar with the tests necessary to provide the best possible evidence in court, and with the problems which such evidence presents. Such a practice would appear to be advisable throughout Canada, but at the very least all hospitals should be encouraged to provide fully qualified staff for such examinations. Hospitals should also provide training programmes designed to familiarize staff with the necessary

procedures for obtaining proper evidence and for providing a supportive, non-judgmental milieu for the victim.

We also found a lack of uniformity in such practices as making a
future appointment with the victim to test whether or not she had
contracted venereal disease or become pregnant as a result of the
rape. We believe that, subject only to the consent of the victim,
antibiotics should be routinely administered to combat any initial
infection that may have occurred, that standard V.D. tests should be
run, and that the victim should be assured that she can have an
abortion if she has become pregnant because of the rape. Some hospitals provide victims with "morning-after pills"—large doses of
abortifacient hormones—as a protection against possible pregnancy,
but they frequently do so without warning the victim about their
side-effects. We believe that these pills should be provided if the
victim wants them, but only after she has been told about the possible side-effects.

Some hospitals also ask the victim if she would like to receive
follow-up psychiatric assistance. Again, we believe that such services should be made available to the victim if she wants them, and
that hospitals should be organized to provide this support. However,
we do not believe that every rape victim requires this type of treatment, and would recommend against any procedure that puts pressure on a victim to pursue it. A rape victim should not be made to
believe that she must and will need psychiatric help, since this expectation only serves to entrench the view that she *ought* to feel guilty
and ashamed of what has happened to her, whether she does or not.
But she should certainly be made aware that such services are available to her if she wants them, either at the time of the rape, or in the
future.

Following their initial interview with the complainant, the
police may decide that the rape report is unfounded, and the matter
will be dropped. Otherwise, they will continue their investigation
and the victim will be interviewed a number of times by the detectives assigned to her case. Their investigation may last for weeks, or
even months, depending on how easily a suspect can be apprehended. They will ask the victim to help prepare composite draw-
ings of the suspect, or to pick him out of crowds or police line-ups.[3]

Once the police believe that a rape has occurred, and that there is
a reasonable chance of successful prosecution, they will leave no stone

unturned in their effortsto arrest the rapist. In many cases, months and months of painstaking legwork will be spent trying to track down the rapist. All available leads will be followed; key locations will be watched; neighbours and employers will be visited; license plates will be traced; car repair and body shops will be checked. If the rapist has given the victim any information about himself, it will be investigated carefully.

Nor is the police role limited to finding and charging the rapist. Typically, the same team of detectives will remain with the case throughout the preliminary hearing and trial. They will be the victim's main source of support within the judicial system. If the victim is given any preparation at all for the courtroom experience, it is usually provided by the police rather than the crown attorneys. These detectives may explain to the victim the various procedures, issues and terms that will arise. They will also try to prepare her for the difficult questions of cross-examination. They know that an uncontrolled display of emotion can do more to sway a jury to the victim's point of view than any amount of rationally delivered testimony, and will encourage her to express herself freely, so that her testimony at trial closely mirrors her original reactions to the offence. But since the trial usually takes place seven to eight months after the rape itself, it is almost inevitable that the victim will feel some emotional detachment from the event. Indeed, it is in her interest that she should. This dilemma is just one of the many problems that the victim will encounter as a result of appearing in court.

If a suspect is arrested, he will be charged with one or more offences. One of the greatest difficulties with rape cases is the problem of finding suspects who may be completely unknown to their victims. Often, when a suspect is finally arrested, as many as five or six rapes will be traced to him, covering a period of months or even years. Though he may be responsible for several offences, his case usually goes to trial on one count only—the one most likely to lead to successful prosecution.

The first step in the court process is the preliminary hearing. The defendant's lawyer and the crown attorney will set a date for the preliminary, which usually takes place from one to five months after the rape. In the meantime, the suspect will probably be released on bail.[4] The preliminary hearing takes place before a judge without a jury. Its function is to assess the facts of the case to see if there is sufficient evidence against the accused to warrant a trial. The accused will be represented by defence counsel, and a crown prosecutor will present the evidence against the accused. At trial and at the preliminary, the rape victim is the main witness for the prosecution, and the defence lawyer may ask her any of the questions he is allowed to put to her at trial.

At this point, it is necessary to discuss briefly some of the courtroom procedures that can affect the outcome of a rape case. Since "consent" is a key legal element of rape, the defence strategy will often be to discredit the victim's credibility. If the defence can show that the victim is not the kind of person who can be believed, then her claim that she did not consent to this particular act of sexual intercourse will be thrown into question. In his attempt to undermine the victim's credibility, the defence lawyer may introduce information about her character, which has nothing to do with whether or not she was raped by the accused, but may prejudice the jury against her.

It is the responsibility of the crown attorney and the presiding judge to prevent this kind of evidence from being used against the victim. The prosecution and the defence both have the right to object to certain lines of questioning when their witnesses are being cross-examined. When defence lawyers ask rape victims about their past sexual experiences, for example, crown attorneys should protest to the presiding judge that these questions are irrelevant.

Judges have the discretionary power to disallow certain evidence and lines of questioning. If a rape victim feels that she is being harassed by the defence lawyer, and that the crown is not objecting to irrelevant questions when he should, she may appeal directly to the judge for a ruling on whether she is obliged to answer. The judge may respond supportively to the victim, and her action may also stimulate the crown attorney to greater vigilance on her behalf. However, the judge and the crown should monitor the defence lawyer's questions themselves, since a rape victim's intervention may cause the jury to think she has something to hide. Unfortunately, judges and crown attorneys often do not use the powers they have to protect the victim from the unscrupulous methods of defence lawyers. This situation is made even worse by the kind of evidence which is allowed in rape trials.

Two extraordinary rules of evidence apply in rape cases, and their application has led many feminists to conclude that it is the rape victim who is on trial in court. The first allows the defence to question a rape victim about her "respectability" in general and her sexual history in particular. This kind of questioning is allowed on the grounds that it supposedly relates to the victim's general credibility. Can the jury believe her testimony as to the non-consensual nature of this particular act of intercourse, if she has consented to intercourse in the past? No logic can possibly justify the inference that having said "yes" on other occasions makes it less likely that she said "no" on this particular occasion. All of the argued justification for admitting such evidence is pure window-dressing. The point of introducing it is to show that the victim isn't, in fact, the sort of woman who can be raped, since she has already consented to intercourse with other men. The inference is either "Once more doesn't make any difference" or "She wasn't a virgin, so no harm was done". The admissibility of such evidence quite clearly demonstrates that a central feature of a rape trial is the character of the *victim*. This is openly stated in Canadian law. In the case of *Regina v. Greatbanks,* it was decided that evidence which attacked the "chastity or common decency" of the victim should be allowed in court:

> In a case other than rape such evidence would clearly not be admissible. In rape cases, however, special rules applied....showing that she was a woman of loose character or notorious for want of chastity or indecency was, on the authorities, admissible.[5]

The implication is that an "unchaste" woman will sleep with any man. If she says she wasn't willing to sleep with the accused, she must be lying.

The second rule of evidence is the iniquitous "corroboration requirement". With any crime other than rape, the victim's testimony alone is sufficient evidence for a conviction. In a rape trial, the victim's testimony must be corroborated (that is, supported) by other evidence, such as torn clothing or the testimony of an independent witness. This principle has been embodied in the "Instruction to the Jury" described in the old Section 142 of the Criminal Code. This is no longer part of the law, but until recently a judge was required to instruct a jury as follows, at the end of a rape trial:

> If, after considering all the evidence, the arguments of counsel, and my charge, you come to the conclusion that the only evidence that implicates the accused is the evidence given under oath by the

complainant...and if you come to the further conclusion that her evidence has not been corroborated, in a material particular, by evidence that implicates the accused, then and in such circumstances, it is my duty to instruct you that it is not safe to find the accused guilty in the absence of such corroboration, but that you are entitled to find the accused guilty if you are satisfied, beyond a reasonable doubt, that her evidence is true.[6]

If a judge felt that such corroborative evidence had not been presented, he could direct a verdict of "not guilty" to the jury. In any case, he was obliged to say whether or not such evidence had, in his opinion, been introduced. The instruction made it clear that the victim's word, even under oath, was not credible. This instruction is no longer required by law, but some judges will likely continue to comment to the jury upon the need for corroboration. And if this were not enough, the case of *Regina v. Kyselka et al* enshrines the principle that evidence which supports the credibility of the victim is *not* admissible.[7]

The only other area in Canadian law where such a demand for corroboration exists is under the Juvenile Delinquency Act, which requires corroboration of the testimony of minors. Thus, women and children are not to be believed unless their testimony can be supported. Rape is the only criminal offence in which the testimony of one witness, the victim, is considered to be inherently less trustworthy than that of others, notably the accused. The issue of the accused's credibility, on the other hand, is hardly allowed to arise. He is not compelled to take the stand in his own defence, and unless he does, the Crown cannot even introduce evidence about past convictions for rape.[8]

In fact, the instruction to the jury makes it clear that a jury *can* convict on the uncorroborated testimony of the victim, if they are satisfied beyond a reasonable doubt that her evidence is true. However, this provision is often overlooked because of the way in which the instruction is given. Many judges, instead of merely saying that it is "not safe" to convict without corroboration, will say that it is *dangerous* to convict without it.

Because the corroboration requirement is so obviously unjust, it has become the object of legal reform. When the amendments to the Criminal Code became law on April 26, 1976,[9] the judge's instruction to the jury was abolished, and tighter controls were placed on defence lawyers' examination of a rape victim's sexual history. Section 142 of the Criminal Code now reads as follows:

NO QUESTION OF SEXUAL CONDUCT

142. (1) Where an accused is charged with an offence under section 144 or 145...no question shall be asked by or on behalf of the accused as to the sexual conduct of the complainant with a person other than the accused unless

   (a) reasonable notice in writing has been given to the prosecutor by or on behalf of the accused of his intention to ask such question together with particulars of the evidence sought to be adduced by such question and a copy of such notice has been filed with the clerk of the county; and

   (b) the judge, magistrate or justice, after holding a hearing *in camera* in the absence of the jury, if any, is satisfied that the weight of evidence is such that to exclude it would prevent the making of a just determination of an issue of fact in the proceedings, including the credibility of the complainant.[10]

These changes will not, however, solve the problem of a rape victim's prejudicial treatment within the criminal justice system. Abolishing the judge's instruction to the jury is an important reform, but in practice the concept that a rape victim's testimony must be corroborated will remain a powerful tool that defence lawyers can use against rape victims. If a victim's testimony that she has been raped is not supported by other, material evidence, the defence lawyer may argue that her word requires corroboration. He could argue throughout the trial that the victim is not credible, that her testimony cannot stand on its own, and the need for corroboration will be one of the main points of his summation to the jury.

It is very easy for defence lawyers to undermine a victim's credibility by attacking her character. The amendments to the Criminal Code make it more difficult for defence lawyers to question a rape victim about her sexual experiences directly, but the "credibility of the complainant" is still singled out as an important issue in rape trials, and it remains to be seen how individual judges will interpret the new legislation. There is ample scope, under the new legislation, for judges to conduct rape trials on the old footing and to treat questions concerning a victim's sexual history as both relevant and legitimate.[11] As long as questions of this sort are allowed at all, they will inevitably be used to discredit the victim, and to suggest that her testimony concerning the non-consensual nature of the act requires corroboration. But even if these questions were disallowed under any circumstances, defence lawyers could easily undermine a victim's credibility through indirection and innuendo. While the main issue of a rape trial remains the victim's character, these abuses will continue.

Attacks on a rape victim's character are particularly damaging because of the legal concept of "reasonable doubt". Juries are not supposed to convict unless they are persuaded beyond a reasonable doubt that the accused is guilty as charged. Mr. Justice Roach, of the Ontario Court of Appeal, has said:

> By reasonable doubt as to a person's guilt is meant that real doubt...which an honest juror has after considering all the circumstances of the case, and as a result of which he is unable to say: "I am morally certain of his guilt."...It is the necessity for such moral certainty that prevents a jury from testing the guilt of the accused by that standard of doubt which would influence them in their ordinary daily affairs. In our daily affairs we constantly act on probabilities and seldom on moral certainty. It is rudimentary that a jury can never convict simply because they consider that a prisoner is probably guilty.[12]

In a rape trial, "reasonable doubt" is bound to be interpreted very strictly. If the main argument for the defence is that the victim consented to intercourse, then the jury must be convinced beyond a reasonable doubt, not only that the accused forced intercourse upon the complainant, but that she did not consent to it, before they can convict the defendant. The judge's instruction to the jury spells this out very clearly:

> The crown to succeed must prove to your satisfaction beyond a reasonable doubt, that the complainant...did not consent to the acts of which she now complains. There is no onus on the accused to prove that she did consent.[13]

The emphasis on a victim's character, the demand for corroboration, and the way in which the need for proof beyond a reasonable doubt casts the onus on the victim, all work together in a rape trial to weaken the prosecution's case and to make conviction very unlikely.

Though these courtroom procedures and rules of evidence are most significant at the trial itself, they also play an important part in the preliminary hearing. As we mentioned earlier, the defence lawyer may ask the rape victim questions about her background and sexual experiences in the preliminary hearing as well as at trial. While the preliminary is only the first step in the judicial process, it has an immense impact on the victim. It is her first court appearance, and the defence uses it to test the witness, looking for any weaknesses in the Crown's case which will be useful to him at trial. He also uses it to "harden the witness up". If he can cause her to break down emotionally at the preliminary, when there are no jurors present, she will be less likely to break down at trial in front of a jury that might be moved to sympathy. Technically, he is searching for weaknesses in the Crown's case, but practically speaking this means finding out as much about the victim as he can. He will fish for any potentially damaging information in order to destroy her credibility at trial.

The victim is very poorly prepared for these tactics. Frequently, the crown attorney assigned to the preliminary hearing is relatively inexperienced, and may have had no contact whatsoever with the victim prior to the court appearance. More often than not, the crown does not ask the judge for a ruling on certain lines of questioning, even when he could. Nor do most judges use their discretionary powers to protect the victim from irrelevant but prejudicial questions.[14] At trial, of course, the defence may prejudice the jury against the victim simply by asking provocative questions about her background and character. If his questions are allowed at all, the damage is done, even if there is no basis in fact for his insinuations.

The rationale for all this legal flim-flam is that our system of criminal justice is an *adversarial* system, in which the defence is doing a proper job only if he uses any means he can to get his client acquitted. His questions may be indefensible from a moral point of view, even from a factual point of view. He may be quite aware that the judge or the crown attorney could easily stop his line of questioning. But he knows that making the suggestion is often enough. The only way to avoid these abuses in court is to disallow such questioning altogether.

Because the rape victim is inadequately prepared, and because prosecuting crowns and presiding judges are reluctant to use their discretionary powers, defence lawyers are able to use the preliminary as something of a fishing expedition, even though this is precisely what it is not supposed to be. If witnesses were better prepared, and crowns and judges were more willing to use the powers they have, defence lawyers would not have such a tidy catch. They would not be able to come to trial armed with such an array of irrelevant but highly prejudicial flies and lures to flash and dangle before the jury.

The wonder is that any victims proceed beyond the preliminary when they know what is in store for them.

If, at the conclusion of the preliminary hearing, the judge rules that there is sufficient evidence to place the accused on trial, the accused will be formally charged on an indictment which is then submitted to a grand jury.[15] The indictment will include a list of all the offences with which the accused is charged,[16] and a list of all the witnesses who will appear on behalf of the Crown. The function of the grand jury is to examine the indictment, and the witnesses in support of it, in order to ascertain whether it is a "true" or "no" bill—that is, whether there really is enough evidence against the accused to charge him with the offences listed on the indictment. The accused is not required either to attend or to be represented by defence counsel since the purpose of the grand jury is to examine the Crown's case against the accused. However, all of the Crown's witnesses can be questioned, and the rape victim must appear before the grand jury. The grand jury is made up of a presiding judge and seven laypersons, usually male. They can ask the victim any questions they feel are relevant to the charges against the accused. The grand jury usually takes place four to eight weeks after the preliminary hearing. If a "true" bill is returned, the case will be assigned a trial date.[17]

The case now goes to trial, usually four to twelve weeks after the grand jury. Where and how it is tried depends on the accused, who can choose to be tried by judge and jury or by jury alone, either in county court or in the Provincial Supreme Court. He inevitably "elects" (chooses) trial by judge and jury, in the Supreme Court, and he usually pleads "not guilty". He chooses judge and jury because he has a better chance of being acquitted by a jury even if they believe he committed the crime. He knows (or more precisely, his lawyer knows) that a jury's decision will reflect its beliefs not only about the accused, but also about the victim. He chooses the Supreme Court because this lends an aura of great importance to the proceedings, reinforcing the notion that he is being tried for a very serious offence and must be found guilty only if there is no shadow of a doubt that he did it (and that she didn't deserve it). And he pleads "not guilty"—not only because, given current conviction rates, that is clearly the safest plea to make, but also because he usually doesn't believe that he has done anything wrong.

At trial, the victim is subjected to the same sort of questioning she experienced in cross-examination at the preliminary hearing. The defence will probe those areas he feels to be most useful to his case, on the basis of information he obtained at the preliminary. He may have had private detectives dig up as much prejudicial information about her as possible; he may be armed with "expert" witnesses—such as psychiatrists—who will describe the victim's past and present mental state. (Recall, however, that no testimony which would support her credibility is admissible.) Defence counsel will try to suggest that the rape victim is an alcoholic, mentally unstable, addicted to drugs, generally of bad reputation, characteristically "idle" or unemployed, or of doubtful occupational status. In short, he will do everything he can to undermine her "credibility". He will try to show either that she should not be believed, or that she only got what she deserved. His job is to persuade the jury that they should not convict his client, and he will use any means he can to secure acquittal. While no one would want to suggest that he is aided in this pursuit by the crown and the presiding judge, they frequently provide him with very few obstacles.

Usually crown prosecutors who handle rape trials are more experienced than those who handle preliminary hearings, but a problem arises from the lack of continuity between these two events. Often, the trial prosecutor is inadequately briefed by the prosecutor who appeared at the preliminary. Needless to say, this situation does not contribute to the victim's sense of well-being, though she will probably have had at least some contact with the prosecutor before appearing at trial. Only a continuing relationship inspires trust, and the victim normally feels a greater sense of support and trust with the police detectives who have remained with the case from initial investigation to trial.[18]

At the conclusion of the trial, both the prosecution and the defence will make their summations to the jury, and the judge will instruct the jury. All the jury may know is that the offence of rape carries a maximum sentence of life imprisonment. They do not themselves pass sentence, and have no idea of the usual length of sentence. Thus, it is quite possible that they may reach a verdict with the thought firmly in mind that, if they convict, the defendant could get life imprisonment. Precise data on length of sentence will be discussed in the next section of this chapter, but the point can be made here that no one is ever sentenced to anything like that maximum. It is unfair to expect juries to make a fair judgment on the facts of the case when they may be under the misapprehension that they could be sending a man to prison for life. Juries should either be given the power to recommend sentence, or they should be told the likely range of sentence the accused could receive if they find him guilty.

When the jury returns its verdict, and if it is "guilty", the judge will set another date for sentencing. Judges alone pass sentence, and on this date the victim does not need to appear in court. However, even this is not always the end of the matter as far as the victim is concerned. Following sentencing, the case can be appealed, even if only for a reduction in sentence. If the case goes to appeal, the victim may be required to appear, depending on the nature of the appeal. If the appeal results in an order for a new trial, she may have to begin the whole process again. Appeals are sometimes successful; that is, the accused is either acquitted or granted a new trial. The victim will usually not be informed of the appeal's outcome unless, of course, it results in a new trial at which she must appear. As appeals may not be heard until a year or so following the original trial, the whole process involves something like eighteen to twenty-four months before it is finally settled. It is a period in which the victim finds little time for solace and much time to regret reporting the offence at all.

the rapist evades the law

If the judicial system appears to penalize the rape victim, it also appears to deal less harshly with the rapist than our laws against rape might lead us to expect. The myth that rape is treated as a serious crime is effectively undercut by the data on arrests, convictions and sentencing.

Only 58.3% of the 1230 rapes reported in Canada in 1971 were "cleared" by an arrest.[19] In our own study, only 59.5% of the founded rape cases were cleared by arrest,[20] and we must remember that the ease with which a suspect can be arrested is one of the reasons police may classify a case as founded. If we look at both the F and U/PF cases, we find that only 24% of these cases led to an arrest. This figure is somewhat misleading in itself, since classification of a case as unfounded means that no further steps will be taken to apprehend a suspect. Nevertheless, many unfounded cases are problematic precisely because of the difficulty of finding the rapist, and it is reasonable to assume that arrest rates would be even lower if U/PF rapes were classified as founded.

We are well aware that rapists are among the most difficult offenders to locate, and certainly the police will spare no effort in searching for a suspect if they believe that a rape has occurred. The police also try to play a preventive role whenever they can. In several cases which had been classified as unfounded in our study (for what were pretty clearly practical reasons), the police interviewed a suspect at the division station and warned him about the charges that could be laid against him. Nevertheless, the general rate of arrest is very low, even for founded rape cases. It is far from comforting to know that so many rapists are never apprehended, much less convicted.

A rather harsher conclusion, that Canadian society tacitly condones rape, is borne out by an analysis of conviction rates. Of the 119 suspects charged with rape in Canada in 1971,[21] only 65 (54.6%) were convicted.[22] In 1962, the conviction rate for rape in Ontario was 42.0%.[23] Mohr, in his study of rape cases in Metropolitan Toronto, found a conviction rate of only 18.0%.[24] This figure is in line with Glueck's findings in the United States.[25] Our own further research suggests a figure for Ontario of 32.1%, which is higher than Mohr's figure but lower than the national average for 1971 or the Ontario figure for 1962.[26] The statistics vary considerably, but the current highest reported conviction rate for rape or a lesser offence is 51.2%.[27]

These figures are low in at least two senses. First, they are low in comparison with rates of conviction for other criminal offences. The vast majority of persons charged with a criminal offence plead guilty, and the general conviction rate is 86.0%, whatever the plea.[28] But secondly, given the elaborate filtering system which brings only some rape cases to court, the number of convictions for rape represents only a tiny fraction of the number of rapes committed.

Even a cursory look at sentencing reveals a similar contradiction between the theory and the practice of the law. As we have seen, the Criminal Code provides severe penalties for rape; a convicted rapist may theoretically be sentenced to life imprisonment.[29] However, it is very unusual for a convicted rapist to be sentenced to more than ten years in prison.[30] The average sentence is believed to be from five to seven years. With remission and parole, this means that the convicted offender will not likely spend more than eighteen to twenty-four months in prison. National data on the sentencing of sixty-three convicted rapists in 1971 show that sentences ranged from a suspended sentence (in one case) to fourteen years or more (one case). Twenty-three rapists were sentenced to two to five years, twenty-eight to more than five years, and twelve to less than two years. Thus, the average length of sentence in Canada appears to be four to five years.[31] In Ontario, the average sentence for rape between 1970 and 1973 was 4.3 years, and sentences ranged from a minimum of a $250.00 fine to a maximum of twelve years' imprisonment.[32]

These figures do not support the claim that rape is treated as a serious crime in our society. In fact, lengths of sentence for rape are comparable with sentences for robbery.[33] This suggests that a rape is considered to be no more serious than a robbery. We are not advocating stiffer penalties for rape; we share the general skepticism about the effectiveness of the penal system, and have no reason to believe that prison either deters or rehabilitates rapists. Until the penal system is replaced with something else, however, it would appear to us that the penalties for rape ought to reflect our supposed moral judgments about the gravity of the crime. Otherwise, we should stop claiming that we condemn rape as a serious offence.

the filtering process

The progress of a rape case through the criminal justice system reflects a highly selective process of elimination. Only a fraction of all rapes are reported; only a fraction of reported rapes are classified as founded; only a fraction of founded cases lead to an arrest; and only a fraction of suspects arrested are convicted. Our own study provided us with a vivid illustration of how few rapes ever lead to trial and conviction. We believed that a rape had most likely occurred in 104 of the 116 cases we studied. If only 40% of all rapes are reported (the highest of all estimated reporting rates), then these 104 reported rapes represented the approximately 260 rapes which actually occurred. The police classified only 42 of the 116 reported rapes as founded, and arrested 32 suspects. Given an average conviction rate of 51.2%, approximately 17 suspects were probably convicted. Thus only 17 out of approximately 260 rapists are likely to be convicted in Metropolitan Toronto—only 7%. That is the highest estimate that any of the figures, at any stage of the process, would justify. As such, it stands as something of a monument to injustice, and a serious indictment of our criminal justice system.

The filtering process begins with the rape victims who decide not to report the offence. Though this stage may appear to be outside of the judicial system, the victim's decision not to report often stems directly from her knowledge of what may happen to her in court, and from her awareness of social attitudes towards rape which the courts reflect.

The second stage of the filtering process is police classification of a case as founded or unfounded. It is important to understand, however, that police classification of a case as unfounded does not always mean that the police do not believe that a rape has occurred. More frequently, the police use the "unfounded" classification to screen out cases which will be difficult to prosecute. The rapist may appear very difficult to trace; the case may lack the corroborative evidence needed at trial; the victim's character and history may suggest to the police that she will not make a favourable impression on the jury. Or, simply, the rape victim may be a "hostile witness" who refuses to co-operate with the police.

When we reviewed the 74 unfounded cases, we attempted to determine which kind of reason had motivated police classification. It was by no means easy to make such judgments. Many reports gave no reason at all for ultimate classification. At times, however, it was obvious that a case had been classified as unfounded because the victim was unwilling to testify, or because the reporting officer felt that the case would be a "bad" case from the point of view of prosecution. In other cases, it appeared that the police did not believe that the complainant had actually been raped. In still others, both kinds of reasons had apparently determined classification. While no precise figures are possible, we would estimate that fully two-thirds of the unfounded classifications had arisen, at least partially, from pragmatic considerations of what the likely outcome would be if such cases proceeded to trial.

This leaves one-third, or approximately 24 cases, which were not classified as unfounded for such practical reasons. However, we have concluded that only 12 reported rapes were genuinely unfounded. The suspicion arises that in the remaining 12 cases, individual police officers viewed the victim and her complaint through their own biased judgment. While no police reports demonstrated clear-cut bias, some reports did indicate that police officers share general prejudices about "appropriate" behaviour for women, and that these prejudices affect classification of rape reports.

But what of the cases which the police do decide to push forward? In classifying a case as founded, the police have an eye not merely on the past, but on what is yet to come. They have an interest in pursuing only those cases which have a fair chance of conviction, because rates of police efficiency are based in part on the ratio of the number of charges laid to the number of convictions achieved. Both the Police Department and the Office of the Crown Attorney will do as much as possible to ensure the best outcomes for their cases. The police are unwilling to push a case to prosecution if they know an acquittal is likely, because a great deal of time, energy and public money goes into the preparation of each case. Also, the police know just how difficult it is to achieve conviction in a rape case, and how reluctant crown attorneys are to prosecute problematical cases.

As a result, the police are forced to operate as an elaborate screening device, a highly selective filter, through which only the "best" of even the founded cases proceed. They try to give the Crown only those cases in which conviction is at least possible. There is no reason to assume that the police would not bring forward more cases, despite the difficulties of prosecution, if their work were supported by further phases of the criminal justice system. But the impetus for such change must come from the Crown.

Clearly, the police should not have to cater to the prejudices of juries in this way. They feel they have been placed in an ambigous and compromising role, and they do not like it. No one knows better than the police just how affected victims are by rape; no one is closer both to the victims and to the event, and no one in the judicial system has a greater interest in seeing offenders prosecuted and convicted. The police feel deep bitterness and resentment over low conviction rates and the treatment of victims at trial. At times, the police are even more frustrated and angry at the tactics of defence counsel than the victims themselves. But if they did not screen out the majority of rape cases, conviction rates would be even lower than they are, further entrenching the belief that most rape charges are false, and that police officers should find better things to do with their time than investigate bogus rape cases.

The fault of the present situation does not lie with the police, but with all of society. The police are called upon to defend the interests of rape victims, but must do so without fundamentally challenging the myths and prejudices which undermine the victim and benefit the accused. Until other social and governmental agencies, including the

Crown, are prepared to take on the task of educating the men and women who become jurors, lawyers, judges, as well as police officers, then the police have little choice but to act as they do.

Thus, police classification of a rape report as unfounded should not necessarily be interpreted as meaning that the police do not believe a rape has occurred. In the interest of generating more meaningful statistics, we would recommend that the police introduce further categories into their classification to distinguish the genuinely unfounded cases from those which cannot be pursued because of the victim's unwillingness to testify, or because of the overwhelming problems which they present for the prosecution. Refined reporting techniques would also compel police officers to state clearly why they are classifying cases as they are.

In the next three chapters of this book, we will present the results of our research to construct a picture of the crime, the rapist, and the victim. We will also analyze specific variables to determine the nature and extent of their influence upon police classification of rape reports. This discussion should both illustrate and clarify the general points we have made so far concerning police classification, and the treatment of rape victims within the judicial system.

4
the crime

In Canada, as elsewhere, the reported incidence of rape is increasing. The number of reported rapes went from 449 in 1961[1] to 1230 in 1971,[2] an increase of 174% in ten years. Moreover, this increase is an absolute one, which cannot be explained merely by the growth in population during the same period. In Metropolitan Toronto, reported rape increased 76% over the five-year period 1969-1973.[3]

It has been argued that these figures indicate only that more rapes are being reported, and not necessarily that more rapes are being committed. Since reports of rape constitute our only data for estimating how often rape occurs, this argument is difficult to refute. However, it is the general opinion of all those connected with law enforcement or research in the area, that rape is still one of the most under-reported offences. This was the conclusion of Hood and Sparks, for example, in a good discussion of the general problem of unrecorded and unreported crime.[4] Medea and Thompson, in the United States, found that only 30% of rape victims in their study had reported the offence.[5] In Canada, the most knowledgeable and most frequently heard "guesstimate" is that for every ten rapes committed, between 1 and 4 are reported.[6] And a Toronto psychiatrist, whose clients include a large number of rape victims and their husbands, believes that only 1 rape in 25 is reported. Thus, estimates of reporting rates go from a high of 40% to a low of 4%. This means that at least 2.5 rapes and as many as 25 rapes occur for every one that is reported. Reported rapes are only the tip of the iceberg.

time and location of offence

Rape is essentially a nocturnal crime,[7] and most rapes take place in the warmer months.[8] We found no significant weekly pattern for the occurrence of the crime, though many other studies have noted that rape is most frequently committed on weekends.[9]

Our data on the location of the offence also supports many of the findings of previous rape research. Rape is usually pictured as a street crime, occurring in dark alleys, parks or parking lots, but many studies have shown that these encounters constitute only a minority of all rape cases.[10] In New York City, for example, 71.7% of the rapes studied took place in some sort of private dwelling. Our results were not nearly so conclusive, but we found that 55.0% of the F and 51.7% of the U/PF rapes had taken place in the private domain. (See table 1.)

It is interesting to look closely at the location of the offence in terms of police classification. When we compare the figures for F and U/PF cases, a significant pattern emerges. Rape reports tended to be classified by the police as founded if the offence had taken place in the victim's residence. In every other category of location, the majority of reports were classified as unfounded, and this trend was most marked for rapes that occurred in the offender's residence. Fully 63.2% of rapes which occurred in the victim's residence were classified as founded, compared with only 28.0% of rapes which occurred in the offender's residence. A victim's report was also more likely to be classified as unfounded if the rape took place in another residence, a vehicle, a public building, street or park. This suggests that the specific location of a rape offence is a significant variable in determining police classification.

If a rape victim has willingly gone to the offender's residence following an initial contact somewhere else, there is less likelihood that a jury will believe that she has been raped since such voluntary prior conduct leads to a presumption that she "enticed" or "provoked" the offender. No one knows better than the police just how

TABLE 1
LOCATION OF OFFENCE

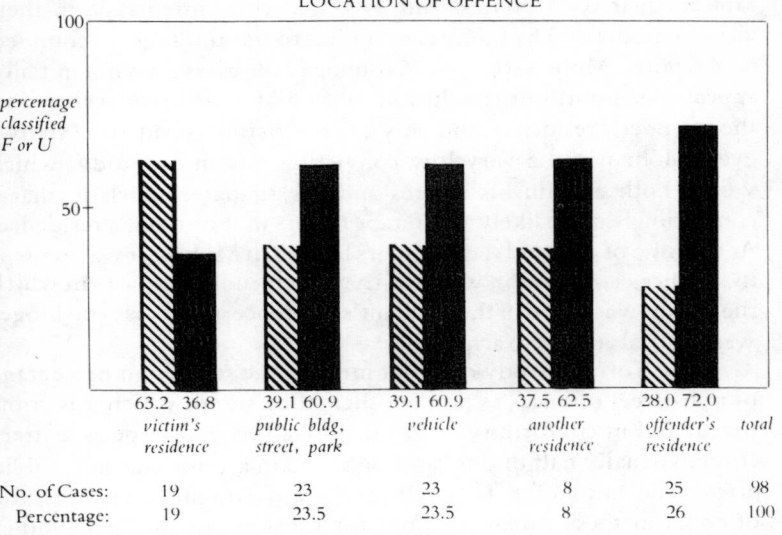

	victim's residence	public bldg, street, park	vehicle	another residence	offender's residence	total
	63.2 36.8	39.1 60.9	39.1 60.9	37.5 62.5	28.0 72.0	
No. of Cases:	19	23	23	8	25	98
Percentage:	19	23.5	23.5	8	26	100

NOTE: No information was available in 2 F and 4 U/PF cases.

▨ percentage classified as founded
■ percentage classified as unfounded by the police,
and as unfounded/possibly founded by Clark/Lewis

As we will be presenting the data for a number of variables in the above manner, some explanation is in order. The two bars for each category of location show what percentage of reported rapes in that category were classified by the police as founded or unfounded, and the exact percentages are written immediately below the bars. The numbers below the category headings (for example, "victim's residence") represent the total number, and the percentage, of reported rapes in each category. Thus, 23 (or 23.5%) of reported rapes occurred in a vehicle. Of these 23 cases, 39.1% were classified as F and 60.9% as U. By multiplying the percentage by the number of cases in the category, the number of F or U cases within each category can be determined. For example, 60.9% or 14 (23 times 60.9%) of the reported rapes which occurred in a vehicle were classified by the police as unfounded (and by us as unfounded/possibly founded).

difficult it is to obtain a conviction in such cases and just how difficult it is for the victim to maintain her innocence in the face of evidence as to such prior conduct. This is clearly reflected in police classification.

The results of other studies provided significant support for our hypothesis that the judicial system discriminates against the victim who is raped in her assailant's residence. McCaldon, in his study of

30 convicted rapists, found that 11% of these men had committed rape in their own homes, and 25% had committed rape in their victims' homes.[11] His figures are similar to our findings for founded rape reports. Mohr's study of 26 founded rape cases does not initially appear to support our conclusion, since 6 of these cases occurred in the offender's residence, and only 2 in the victim's residence.[12] However, Mohr noted a very low conviction rate in his study, which would both explain his figures and substantiate our claim that a conviction is more likely when rape occurs in the victim's residence. At the time of our study, eight years later than Mohr's, it was evident that police classification was effective in screening out cases in which the victim was raped in the assailant's residence; these cases no longer went to trial and led to acquittals.

The Toronto study does not indicate the same high percentage of non-street offences as do the other studies with which it is compared, and in conformity with the public image of rape as a street crime, virtually half of our cases occurred in a vehicle or in a public place. The ratio of F to U/PF cases was roughly the same for offences in these categories, and for those occurring in "another residence". The "public" nature of the location of rape does not, then, seem to be a significant variable in determining police classification. However, it may well be that the *kind* of public location, and the nature of the initial contact between victim and offender, do play a role in police perceptions. This is a matter for further investigation. As can be seen from table 1, the majority of street offences occur in a vehicle. It was our impression, on the basis of comments made on the General Occurrence Reports, that where the initial contact between victim and offender occurred because the victim had been hitch-hiking, or because she had willingly accepted a ride from a stranger (even where he made the first approach), there was a greater likelihood that the police would classify the offence as unfounded. The reason for this, again, is that even where they themselves believe a rape has occurred, the police know that such cases will not be easy to prosecute successfully. Thus, rape may well be even more of a street crime than the present study indicates.

When rape occurs in a private dwelling, the question of whether or not the victim consented to be in the offender's residence is clearly a significant variable in police classification and, one would suspect, in the final outcome of the cases which do proceed to preliminary hearing and trial. The selection process appears to exclude many such cases from going further in the legal process, and to lead to fewer convictions when they do. Thus, it may well be that there is also much more rape which occurs in the private domain than appears evident from the present data. Only further investigation of how many rapes occur as a result of hitch-hiking and accepting rides from strangers, can tell us how much rape is really street crime; and only further investigation of how many rapes occur in situations where the victim consented to some initial contact, can tell us how much more rape is essentially committed in private. What is clear, however, is that it is the prior behaviour of the *victim,* and not the behaviour of the accused, which plays a decisive role in the subsequent fate of rape cases.

TABLE 2
PRESENCE OF ALCOHOL

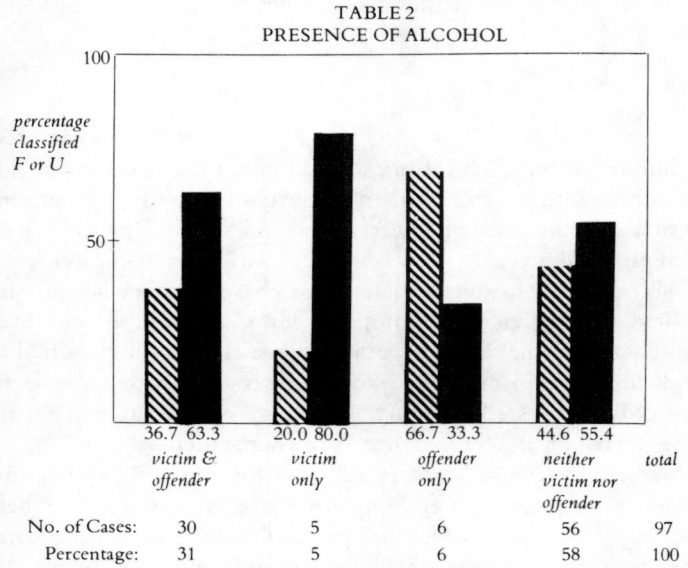

	victim & offender	victim only	offender only	neither victim nor offender	total
	36.7 63.3	20.0 80.0	66.7 33.3	44.6 55.4	
No. of Cases:	30	5	6	56	97
Percentage:	31	5	6	58	100

NOTE: No information was available in 1 F and 1 U/PF cases. In 1 case the victim was given "some substance" by the offender. In 1 case the victim alone had used drugs, and in 3 cases both the victim and the offender had used drugs.

▨ percentage classified as founded
■ percentage classified as unfounded by the police, and as unfounded/possibly founded by Clark/Lewis

use of alcohol

Whether the victim or the offender had been drinking was also a significant factor in determining police classification. (See table 2.) A victim was unlikely to have her report classified as founded if she had consumed alcohol prior to the offence. This variable was even more important, however, if the first impression gained by the police officer was that the victim had been drinking to excess. In such cases, no victim had her case classified as founded. This will be discussed more fully in the next chapter.

A less striking, but still significant relationship was seen in those cases where the offender alone had been drinking. In such situations, a majority (66.7%) of complaints were classified as founded. This classification may be a comment on male behaviour as well. It is more believable (to the courts and the police) that an inebriated man would commit a violent crime such as rape.

use of violence

According to the legal definition, sexual intercourse is rape only if it occurs either without the woman's consent, or with her consent where that consent is obtained through fraud, or through the use or threat of physical force. In the vast majority of cases, some evidence of force is necessary to substantiate a rape charge; otherwise, no one will believe that the victim did not consent. Generally, the victim is more likely to be believed, her report is more likely to be classified as founded, and her rapist is more likely to be convicted, if some form of violence is manifested in the act. Rapists may use weapons, physical force, verbal or non-verbal threats to coerce their victims.

The term "weapon" is very difficult to define. Chappell and Singer, for example, classified "physical force" as a weapon in their study of rape. We did not feel that physical force fell into the same category as a gun, a knife, or a crowbar, which would prove the victim's lack of consent much more convincingly at trial. When completing that part of the General Occurrence Report entitled "weapon", the Metropolitan Toronto police frequently entered the word "penis". While it may be true that this is, indeed, "the weapon" from the victim's point of view, it clearly cannot be considered the same kind of weapon as a gun or a knife. In our study, weapons were mentioned in 13.5% of the cases studied. (See table 3.) Knives, mentioned in 9.6% of these cases, were the weapons most commonly used by rapists. The data available to us was extremely inadequate, and it is not clear that a weapon was not used in the remaining cases; therefore, the figures for "weapons used" must be taken as minimums. However, it is significant that 71.4% of cases involving the use of a weapon were classified as founded, and 64.4%

TABLE 3

OFFENDERS' USE OF WEAPONS

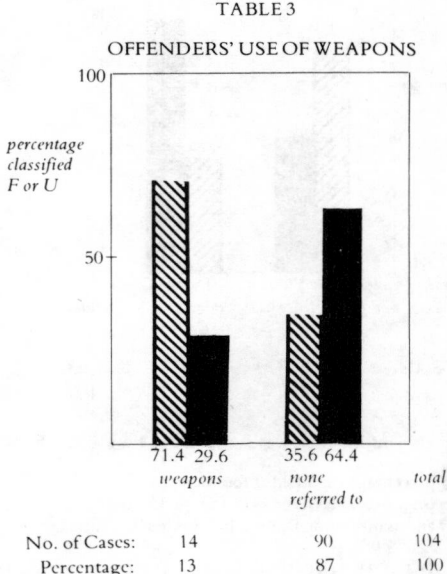

| No. of Cases: | 14 | 90 | 104 |
| Percentage: | 13 | 87 | 100 |

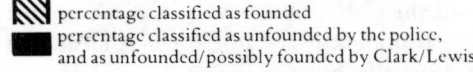

percentage classified as founded
percentage classified as unfounded by the police,
and as unfounded/possibly founded by Clark/Lewis

of cases where no weapon was involved were classified as unfounded.

Physical violence to the victim occurred in 32.0% of the cases studied. (See table 4.) The victim was punched, slapped or kicked in 17.0% of these cases, choked in 8.0%, badly beaten in 3.0%, wounded (cut and bitten) in 3.0% and rendered unconscious in 1.0%. It is apparent from the data that visible evidence of physical injury encourages police to classify a report as founded. More violence of each kind occurred in the F than in the U/PF cases, and a total of 62.5% of cases in which the rapist displayed physical violence were classified as founded.

TABLE 4

OFFENDERS' USE OF PHYSICAL VIOLENCE

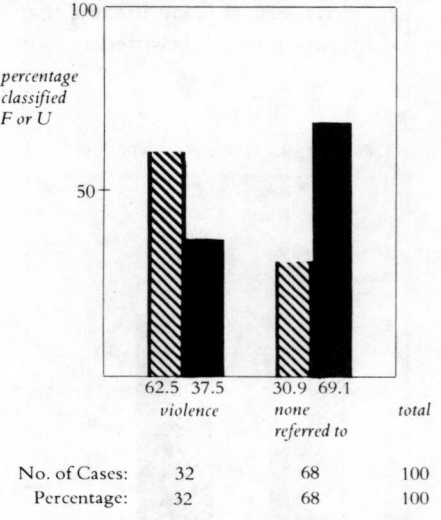

	violence	none referred to	total
	62.5 37.5	30.9 69.1	
No. of Cases:	32	68	100
Percentage:	32	68	100

NOTE: No information was available in 1 F and 3 U/PF cases.

▨ percentage classified as founded
■ percentage classified as unfounded by the police,
and as unfounded/possibly founded by Clark/Lewis

Police were also more likely to classify a case as founded if the rapist made verbal threats to his victim. Threats of one sort or another were made in 37.1% of the cases studied, and 61.1% of these were classified as founded. (See table 5.) It is clear that those who threaten violence usually mean what they say, but since the victim frequently submits under these threats, it is impossible to estimate how much further violence would occur if she did not.

The offenders in our study were less violent than those studied by McCaldon, who reports that force was used in 84% of his cases, and threatened in the remaining 16%.[13] As his study was of convicted rapists, it is not surprising that his figures should be high. The actual or threatened use of violence affects police classification because, ultimately, it affects jury decisions. The greater the degree of violence the more likely a jury is to believe that the victim did not consent to intercourse, and that the commission of the crime placed her at serious risk.

TABLE 5
OFFENDERS' USE OF VERBAL THREATS

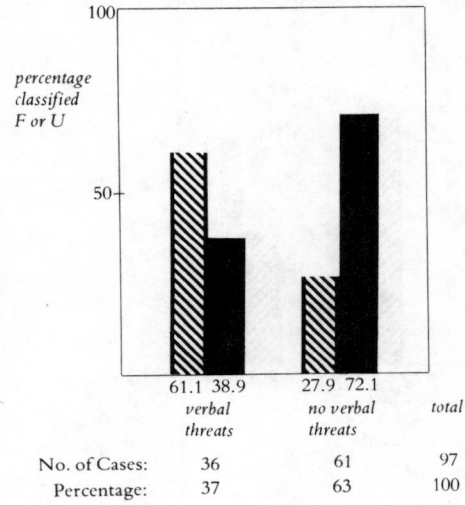

	verbal threats	no verbal threats	total
	61.1 38.9	27.9 72.1	
No. of Cases:	36	61	97
Percentage:	37	63	100

NOTE: No information was available in 3 F and 4 U/PF cases.

▨ percentage classified as founded
■ percentage classified as unfounded by the police, and as unfounded/possibly founded by Clark/Lewis

other sexual acts

Often a sexual assault will include other sexual acts besides that of vaginal penetration. We found that other sexual acts, including fellatio, cunnilingus, oral copulation, anal intercourse, self-masturbation by the offender, and victim masturbation of the offender, occurred in 23.3% of the cases studied. (See table 6.) Fellatio was the most common, occurring in 47.8% of these cases. In themselves, of course, such acts are not forms of violence. But in the rape situation, where they are forced upon an unwilling victim, they contribute to an over-all atmosphere of coercion and fear. If other sexual acts occur which the jury is likely to see as acts to which the victim would not consent, then they are more likely to believe that she would not consent to sexual intercourse either. It is not surprising, therefore, that the police classified 60.9% of such cases as founded.[14]

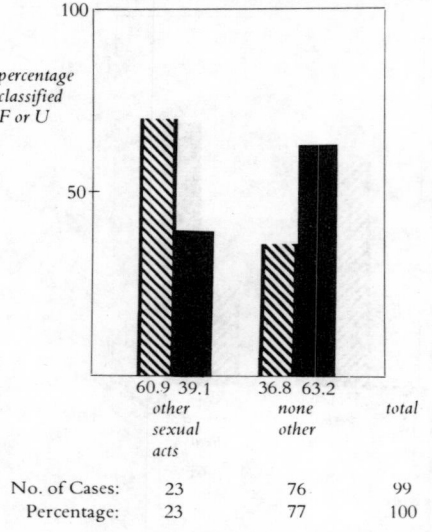

TABLE 6

OCCURRENCE OF OTHER SEXUAL ACTS

percentage classified F or U

	other sexual acts	none other	total
	60.9 39.1	36.8 63.2	
No. of Cases:	23	76	99
Percentage:	23	77	100

NOTE: No information was available in 5 U/PF cases.

▨ percentage classified as founded
■ percentage classified as unfounded by the police,
   and as unfounded/possibly founded by Clark/Lewis

other crimes

The rape studies done by Amir, and by Chappell and Singer, both consider how often other crimes accompany rape. Amir found that 4% of the cases in his study involved what he termed an "explosive rape". This kind of rape occurred after another crime—usually robbery or burglary—had been committed. In another 6% of his cases, the victim was robbed after she had been raped.[15] The New York City study revealed an even larger percentage of "felony-rapes", as Amir refers to them. In this study, 6% of the rape victims were assaulted following the commission of another offence, and 19% were the victims of robbery or burglary after they had been raped.[16] In 12.5% of the cases which we studied, theft occurred as well as rape. There was, however, one important difference between our findings and Amir's. In our study, all but one theft occurred *after* the rape itself. There was no evidence of "explosive rape" as an afterthought following the commission of another offence. On the contrary, it appeared that these thefts were usually incidental to the rape. Most of these thefts involved small amounts, ranging from $5.00 to $65.00, and one rapist returned the money to his victim when she said she needed it.

Theft occurred in 21.4% of the founded cases, and in only 4.9% of the unfounded/possibly founded cases. Police are more inclined to classify a reported rape as founded when it is accompanied by theft, simply because the recovery of stolen goods constitutes corroboration of the victim's testimony, and lends more weight to the entire case.

victim-offender relationships

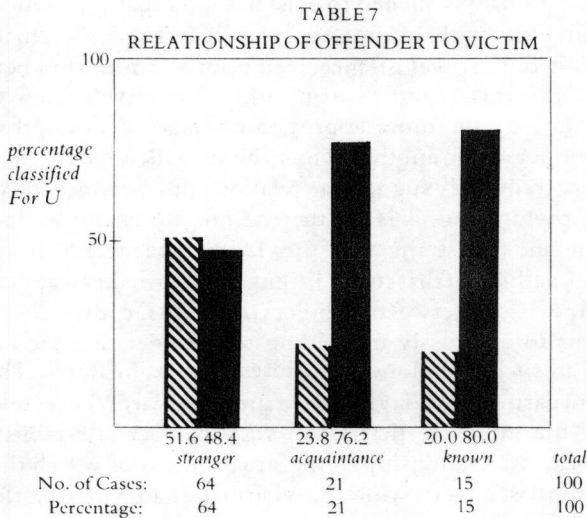

TABLE 7
RELATIONSHIP OF OFFENDER TO VICTIM

	stranger	acquaintance	known	total
	51.6 48.4	23.8 76.2	20.0 80.0	
No. of Cases:	64	21	15	100
Percentage:	64	21	15	100

NOTE: No information was available in 1 F and 3 U/PF cases.

▨ percentage classified as founded
■ percentage classified as unfounded by the police, and as unfounded/possibly founded by Clark/Lewis

Table 7 gives a breakdown of victim–offender relationships prior to the commission of the offence, utilizing three categories:

1. *Known* The victim knew the offender well before the occurrence.

2. *Acquaintance*. The victim did not know the offender well, but had met him *prior* to the situation out of which the rape developed, or had knowledge of him through mutual friends or general reputation.

3. *Stranger*. The offender was either a complete stranger to the victim, or someone whom she had just met in the situation out of which the rape developed.

The way in which we've applied these categories makes it all but impossible and certainly meaningless to compare our findings with those of most other studies. However, we believe that ours was the only adequate method for assessing the real relationship between victim and offender. Other studies have, we believe, distorted the picture of relationships alleged to exist in rape situations. One of the greatest difficulties with those offences labelled as "rape", is that since rape is considered a *sexual* offence, it implies a relationship between two persons. In this, it differs from other assaultive crimes which merely conjure up the more appropriate image of an unprovoked attack by one person on another. Thus, the alleged "sexual" character of the offence frequently suggests a "relationship" between the victim and offender which simply is not there. Amir, for example, does not classify someone as a "stranger" to the victim if she met him in a bar, at a party, or something of that sort.[17] Failing to do so makes it appear that far fewer rapes occur between strangers than is in fact the case.

It seems to us grossly misleading to consider that the contact established in such situations constitutes a "relationship". The fact that bars and parties are today standard meeting places for people does not justify the inference that when such contact is established it instantly creates a relationship. If the situation out of which the rape emerges is the first contact which the victim has had with the offender, and if she has had no prior knowledge of him through previous contacts, mutual friends, or general reputation, then that male is a stranger to that female. That he uses this contact to create a situation in which the victim may later be raped merely indicates a certain amount of *savoir faire*. Doubtless these meetings frequently result in a mutually favourable outcome; not all cases of establishing contact in these ways lead to rape. The woman may be as eager for such contact as the man, and she may or may not be eager for the contact to result in sexual intercourse. While it may be rare for men who meet women in these ways not to hope for intercourse as the ultimate outcome, it is by no means the case that all women who make such contact with men wish anything more than friendship, or companionship which falls short of intercourse. Most men may even have an *expectation* of intercourse, but all women certainly do not. The degree to which women can judge men on the basis of both their own expectations and those of the men involved, is a measure of their experience and maturity. Many rapes are simply the result of bad judgment. A woman may have no desire for, or expectation of, sexual intercourse, and believe that even if the man does, he will not force her. The question in all such cases is whether such male expectations are *justified*, and not simply whether they exist.

The degree to which men may have such expectations, independent of what is actually happening in a particular situation, is a measure only of the extent to which their consciousness of themselves in relation to women is determined by purely abstract principles of male superiority, aggressiveness, and the right to male domination. It does not relate to the legitimacy of those expectations, as based on the real behaviour of the women with whom they come in contact. The stronger the man's conception of himself as superior, aggressive and dominant, the stronger his complementary conception of women as inferior, passive and submissive. He is more likely both to expect sexual intercourse, and to believe that rape is only seduction accomplished by more or less force, depending on the particular nature of the woman involved. For men of this type, *any* behaviour on the part of woman is "provocative". If she says "no", or protests either verbally or physically, her behaviour is taken as an indication that she "likes it better" with force. It is not taken, as it should be, as a rejection of his advances based on her own desires and her own right to be a self-determining human personality.

But seduction is not rape, and rape is not seduction. The fact that some men simply do not take "no" for an answer does not obliterate the real distinction that exists between them; it merely indicates the degree to which some men are total prisoners of sex-role stereotyping. And the fact that some women misjudge the extent to which particular men are so imprisoned, does not make them responsible for their own sexual assault. Nor does the fact that prior contact was established in a less rather than a more coercive situation indicate that the woman has given rise to legitimate or justified expectations. It is difficult to judge strangers, and that is just the problem. But that such first meetings are meetings between strangers is incontrovertible, and the fact that there has been such a meeting certainly should not obliterate the stranger-to-stranger status that exists between victim and offender. When such a distinction is drawn, it becomes readily apparent that more rape occurs between strangers than most studies indicate, and that the failure to classify such events as stranger-to-stranger encounters is a mark of the insensitivity of researchers, and not of the nature of the events.

However, lest it be argued that using categories in the manner which we have adopted is simply to measure the world in a fashion more advantageous to the victim, experimental data can be gathered to support the view that this is, at least in some clearly ascertainable cases, a more "objective" carving of the joints. (Hard data notwithstanding, it hardly seems fair, even *a priori*, to carve up the world in a fashion clearly more advantageous to the offender.) We found that some of the men who use parties and bars to establish contact with the women whom they later rape, are quite well aware that they are strangers to their future victims; in fact, they take great pains to remain so. By comparing available information on offenders on Records of Arrest with information reported by victims,[18] we discovered that some offenders give their victims false information about such things as their name, employment, age, nationality and marital status. In these cases, at least, it seems clear that the offender does not see himself as establishing a "relationship" of any sort whatsoever, though he may appear to do so to gain the trust of the woman involved.

Such discrepancies also suggest a line of further research. It is often alleged, and indeed is one of the oft-quoted myths, that rape is an unpremeditated crime, born of the spontaneous explosion of uncontrollable male lust. But where offenders deliberately feed false information to their victims, it seems obvious that they know what they intend to do and are already taking steps to avoid detection. A careful analysis of such data is needed to increase our knowledge about the degree and kind of premeditation involved in rape offences. However, the incidence of persistent patterns in the commission of the offence on the part of individual offenders, and the use of strategies designed to make detection and apprehension difficult, certainly suggest that a good many rape offences are fully premeditated, and that the intention to commit rape shapes the circumstances in which it occurs.

In summary, our findings certainly suggest that stranger-to-stranger rape is more common in Toronto than elsewhere, but all that can be concluded is that the figures with which they are compared may not be reliable. When the categories are drawn uniformly, we predict that more rape everywhere will turn out to be of this variety. McCaldon's findings do, however, tend to support our conclusions.[19] In assessing the relationship between victim and offender, he distinguishes five categories: lover, friend, acquaintance, stranger and relative. While he does not outline how these categories are drawn, fully 79% of his cases fall into the "stranger" category. A further 10% fall into the "acquaintance" category, and if he is including here the kind of case in which rape follows some initial contact at a bar or party, then 89% of rapes which he analyzes would fall within the "stranger" category distinguished in the present study. Nevertheless, his figure of 79% compares with our figure of 80% for all founded offences, and is higher than our combined total of 64% for both F and U/PF offences. It should be pointed out, however, that the existence of a stranger-to-stranger status between victim and offender is likely one of the significant variables affecting police classification and conviction, and one would therefore expect to find a higher percentage of such relationships in a study based on convicted rapists.

The most conclusive finding supported by our data is that rape only occasionally occurs between persons very well known to each other. The Toronto data was difficult to classify according to only a general "known" category, because the extent of familiarity —acquaintance as opposed to close friend, for example—was difficult to ascertain from police reports. However, a few general trends were noted from the texts of the General Occurrence Reports. Although a small proportion of rapes occurred within the "close friend" or "boyfriend" category used by Chappell and Singer, it appeared that, in most instances, relationships tended to be more casual; for example, the rapist was a neighbour or family friend.[20]

But even this finding may not reflect the true picture. Under the Canadian Criminal Code, a man cannot rape his own wife; thus, one potential group of "known" rapists are automatically ruled out of court. Further, where there has been a long-standing relationship between the victim and offender, the police are much less likely to classify the offence as founded. If a victim has had intercourse with an offender prior to the rape, for example, she is very unlikely to be believed. One certainly cannot rule out the fact that many such victims are themselves aware that they are not likely to be believed, and therefore do not report the offence.

The difficulty in drawing definitive conclusions about victim-offender relationships shows that we cannot know anything about the nature, or lack of relationships between victims and offenders until we have more accurate data on all rape, rather than only on that which comes to us filtered through the highly selective process of the criminal justice system. The chances are good that one may be raped by a stranger. But they are equally good that one may be raped by a friend or acquaintance. In Medea and Thompson's study, 12% of the rapes studied occurred with "dates", 37% with "acquaintances" and only 33% with "strangers".[21] The fact that much rape occurs between persons known to each other, however, ought not obscure the fact that just as much likely takes place between those who are unknown to each other. Similarly, a victim's prior contact with her assailant should not be construed as "evidence" that rape is an event in which a victim "participates" with someone who is "known" to her. Just as rapists differ, so do their methods of operating. Some men rape their dates and some men rape strangers. But we will know nothing of the true percentages until we know more about those rapes which go unreported.

5
the victim

One of the most striking results of our study was the discovery that a rape victim's background and character strongly influence the way in which her report is classified by the police. It is not the rape victim who commits the offence, but it is very clear from our data that the primary determinants of police classification are variables which describe the victim—her age, her marital and occupational status, her emotional and physical condition when she reports the crime. These are the factors which determine whether a case will proceed further in the criminal justice system, or be dismissed as "unfounded".

For this reason, we will present each victim-related variable with an eye to its effect upon police classification. Wherever possible, we will also provide comparative data from other studies, and data from further research to suggest how these variables can affect the subsequent decision about whether to take reported rape offences to preliminary hearing.

With some variables, such as emotional state, the pattern in police classification is obvious and clear-cut. With others, such as age and marital status, factors appear to reinforce or act in conjunction with one another in affecting the classification of a report. We will present each variable separately, and will also discuss how particular variables appear to act as a constellation of factors which have a significant bearing on police classification. But before beginning our analysis of how different types of victims are treated within the judicial system, we should comment upon the broad range and many types of women who become the victims of rape.

victim's appearance

One of the most common misconceptions concerning rape victims is that they are attractive women who dress in a "provocative", "suggestive" or "enticing" manner. We found no justification for this assumption in our own or other data. Our victims, like any other randomly chosen sample of women, displayed a wide range of physical characteristics and styles of dress. This has also been the finding of other researchers. MacDonald, for example, notes:

> Those who believe that the victim of rape is usually an attractive young girl would be surprised by the procession of the middle-aged and elderly as well as the young, the obese and the slim, the neatly dressed and the bedraggled, the sick, the lame and halt to the interviewing rooms of the detective bureau.[1]

While we have no doubt that the victim's appearance plays a role in police classification, it is also our belief that appearance is only important insofar as it reflects other characteristics—such as age, lifestyle and economic status—which more directly affect classification. There is no evidence whatsoever that any one, or even any number of determinable types of physical appearance or mode of attire single out the rape victim from other women.

Nor does the victim's country of origin appear to be a distinguishing feature of rape victims in general, or a consideration in police classification of rape reports. Over three-quarters of the rape victims in our study were English-speaking, and born in Canada; 38.5% of the victims in this group had their reports classified as founded, in comparison with 45.8% of all other victims.

age

The data concerning age appears much more significant, however, particularly when it is combined with data on marital status and occupation. (A discussion of these three factors will follow the section on "Occupation".)

We found that the majority of victims in our study (58.3%) were relatively young—between 14 and 24 years of age— although it was also true that almost one-third (29.1%) were over 30 years of age. (See table 8.) Amir found similar results: almost one-quarter of the victims in his study were between 15 and 19, and one-third were over 30.[2] But what is more interesting is the distribution of ages which recurs in several Canadian studies. McCaldon found that none of his victims fell within the 26-40 range;[3] Mohr found no victims between 30-34[4] and though 5.8% of the victims in our study were between 30-34, only 1 victim in this age group had her report classified as founded.

This apparent "weeding out" of victims in the young-to-middle adult stage is indeed remarkable, though it is somewhat difficult to determine why additional discrimination against women in this age group occurs. It is, however, a trend which gets worse as cases proceed further in the Canadian criminal justice system. According to Clark, Barr-Carley and Ward, *none* of the victims whose cases reach the level of preliminary hearing are between 30-34 years of age.[5] As we shall discuss later, we believe that age is not the sole variable responsible for this trend, but that age together with marital status and occupation form a cluster of variables which are very influential in determining both police classification and whether cases will proceed further in the judicial system.

The distribution of data also indicates an apparent bias against the very young rape victim. As table 8 shows, only 30.6% of the victims between 14-19 years of age had their reports classified as founded. Bearing in mind that our U/PF category represents those cases which we felt did not display any good reason for the "unfounded" classification, it would appear that the very young victim is discriminated against at the level of police classification. Some reasons for this bias are suggested by remarks made in the General Occurrence Reports.

In a number of cases where the investigating police officer did not believe the victim, the victim was very young and the offence was first brought to the attention of the police by one of her parents—usually

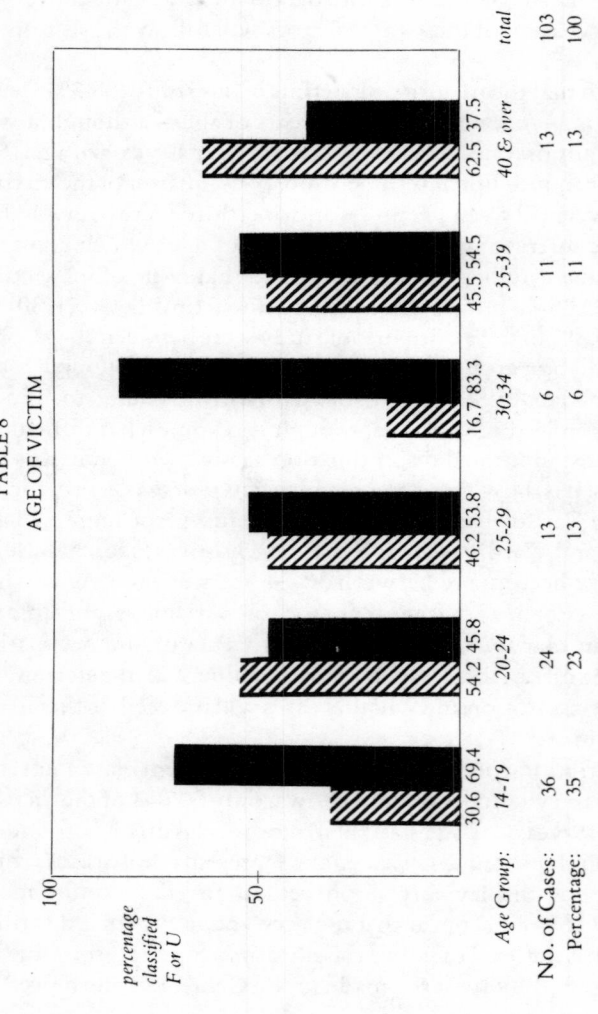

TABLE 8

AGE OF VICTIM

Age Group:	14-19	20-24	25-29	30-34	35-39	40 & over	total
	30.6 69.4	54.2 45.8	46.2 53.8	16.7 83.3	45.5 54.5	62.5 37.5	
No. of Cases:	36	24	13	6	11	13	103
Percentage:	35	23	13	6	11	13	100

NOTE: No information was available in 1 F and 1 U/PF cases, but 1 case included here involved 2 victims.

◪ percentage classified as founded

■ percentage classified as unfounded by the police,
    and as unfounded/possibly founded by Clark/Lewis

her father. The police view seemed to be that the victim had "invented" the rape in order to avoid parental discipline for sexual behaviour to which she had in fact consented. Indeed, among the cases which we agreed were genuinely unfounded, two were of this sort. In both cases the victim had been hostile to the police and unable to tell a consistent story; her behaviour indicated that she felt herself to be trapped in a very difficult situation. It was quite apparent, moreover, that the young woman would face very heavy censure and punishment from her parents for behaviour which they regarded as "promiscuous".

The more ambiguous cases, however, were those in which the police believed that the victim had invented the story, but had no evidence for this judgment beyond either parental disbelief or the victim's general reputation for "promiscuity". The police usually classify a report as unfounded because they know it will not make a "good" case, but in several instances we could not escape the conclusion that the police simply did not believe the victim's story. The cases which most clearly demonstrated this problem were those in which the complainant had had a history of truancy, had been placed in a training school or foster home, or had been known to keep company with other "undesirable" juveniles. In two cases which we examined, there seemed to be no evidence at all that the rape had not occurred, but in each case the victim's mother did not believe her daughter because of her previous "promiscuous" behaviour. One is forced to ask why, in such cases, if there was no rape, and if the parents were not the ones who wished to pursue a charge, the young woman would want to a lay a false complaint—especially within the context of her parents' attitudes towards sexual activity? One could not argue that the victim was seeking revenge, because in both cases the victim did not know her attacker.

It is abundantly evident that parents often use the police to enforce their own judgments. They want the police to break down the victim and to treat her punitively for behaviour which they feel to be "promiscuous". There is a profound and tragic irony in this. Reputations for "promiscuity" need not be based on fact, after all, and "promiscuity" is itself a value judgment—usually imposed by parents, frequently for behaviour which should bear no disapproval. If one has the misfortune of a "bad" reputation or unduly moralistic parents, one should neither be forced to disguise sexual activity as oluntary, nor refused the redress of the law.

It is highly regrettable that the police must become involved in such cases, because in attempting to "break down" the victim's story they cannot help but have the effect of reinforcing conservative parental attitudes, and adding the weight of the judicial system to the judgment of the parents. It is also clear, from our examination of such cases, that parents and police often lose sight of the alleged rape completely, and the result is that the complainant is simply punished for her past behaviour.

The problems surrounding the very young victim are indeed complex, and our view is that these women should be treated rather differently from older rape victims because of the special difficulties posed by parental attitudes and relationships. This is a matter which we shall discuss in detail in the "Recommendations" section of this book. However, as we are beginning to see, age is not a variable which operates on its own to determine police classification. The victims in our study who fell into the 14-19 and 30-34 age groups also tended to share certain marital or socio-economic characteristics, and these characteristics led more directly to the classification of their rape reports as unfounded.

marital status

The majority of rape victims are single: 53.1% of the victims in our study were single, as compared with 57.7% and 78.0% in the studies of Mohr[6] and McCaldon[7] respectively. This finding is hardly surprising, given the youth of over half of the reporting population. But it has a further significance which will be brought out when considering occupational data.

Table 9 shows the marital status of the rape victims in our study, and how the police classified the rape reports of the women in each category. More cases were categorized as U/PF than F for each category of complainant; this difference was slightly more marked for "separated" and "divorced" victims than for "single" or "married" victims. It was in the category of "common law" victims, however, that a bias in police classification most clearly appeared. Fully 78.7% of these cases were classified as U/PF, while only 22.2% were classified as F. Comparative data from Clark, Barr-Carley and Ward's examination of cases reaching preliminary hearing support the finding that single and married rape victims are more likely to be treated seriously within the criminal justice

TABLE 9
MARITAL STATUS OF VICTIM

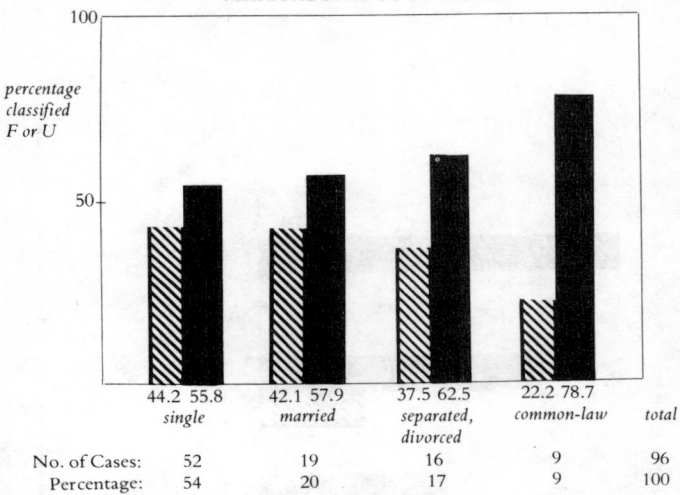

	44.2 55.8	42.1 57.9	37.5 62.5	22.2 78.7	
	single	married	separated, divorced	common-law	total
No. of Cases:	52	19	16	9	96
Percentage:	54	20	17	9	100

NOTE: There were 2 widows, both classified as F. No information was available in 1 F and 6 U/PF cases, but 1 case included here involved 2 victims.

⬚ percentage classified as founded
⬛ percentage classified as unfounded by the police, and as unfounded/possibly founded by Clark/Lewis

system. This study showed that, of the victims whose cases proceeded at least as far as preliminary hearing, 62.5% were single, 25.0% were married, none were separated, 6.3% were divorced, and only 3.1% were living in common-law relationships.[8]

The bias against women who are separated, divorced, or living in common-law relationships is, we believe, one of the factors responsible for the low incidence or total absence of victims in the 30–34 and 35–39 age groups. Of the 6 women in our study who fell into the 30–34 group, 4 were separated, 1 was divorced, and 1 was single. It may be generally true that women in their thirties or late twenties are more likely to be divorced, separated or living in common-law relationships than either younger or older women; this would also account for the very few victims in this age range reported by McCaldon and Mohr. But within our study, the inference was clear: the Canadian criminal justice system tends to dismiss those rape victims who, if of roughly marriageable age, are not living within the approved bonds of

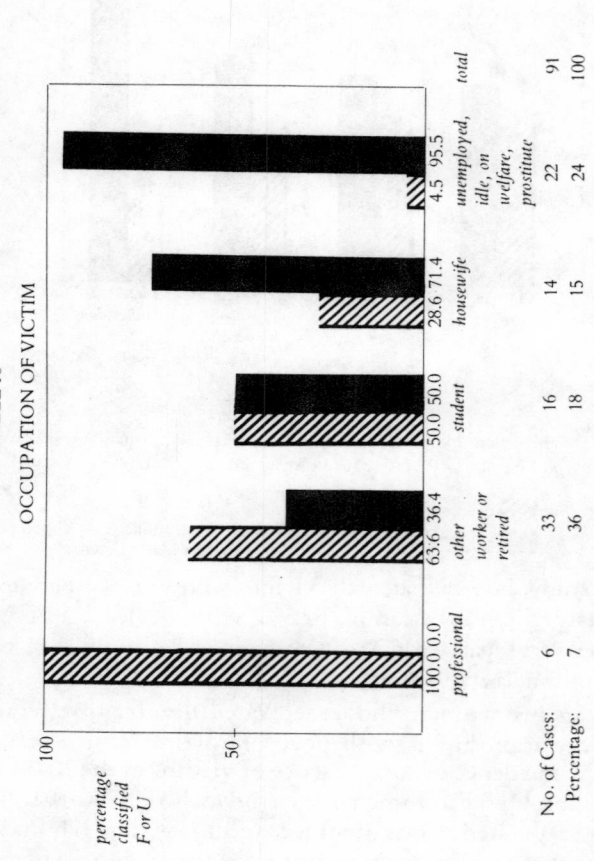

TABLE 10

OCCUPATION OF VICTIM

	professional	other worker or retired	student	housewife	unemployed, idle, on welfare, prostitute	total
percentage classified F or U	100.0 0.0	63.6 36.4	50.0 50.0	28.6 71.4	4.5 95.5	
No. of Cases:	6	33	16	14	22	91
Percentage:	7	36	18	15	24	100

Legend:
- ▨ percentage classified as founded
- ■ percentage classified as unfounded by the police, and as unfounded/possibly founded by Clark/Lewis

NOTE: No information was available in 2 F and 12 U/PF cases, but 1 case included here involved 2 victims.

legal matrimony. And as we shall see, this is also a way of discriminating against women of low socio-economic status.

occupation

Table 10 categorizes the rape victims in our study by occupational group, and it is extremely interesting to analyze police classification within it. Women in the "professional" category were most likely to be believed by the police; 100.0% of them had their cases classified as founded. Other workers and retired women were also quite likely to be believed. This group included 9 clerical workers, 3 factory workers, 7 domestic servants, 3 waitresses, 8 salesclerks and 3 retired women. Students, however, did not fare so well; only 50.0% of their cases were classified as founded. The "housewife" category is interesting in its own right, for only 28.6% of these cases were classified as founded; women in the most usual (and worst paid) of female occupations apparently have only a one-third chance of being perceived as credible rape victims. What is perhaps most striking, however, is the data for victims who were "unemployed", "idle", "on welfare" or "prostitutes". Only 1 case in this category (represented by 1 of the 3 unemployed women in our study) was classified as founded by the police.

relationship of age, marital status and occupation

The data on age, marital status and occupation are most revealing when examined together, for as we have mentioned previously, certain categories within these variables often act as a constellation which affects police classification. At times, it is clear that they are jointly, though perhaps not singly, correlated with the unfounded classification. We have not attempted to tabulate the cross-correlations of age, marital status and occupaton, but with additional, descriptive information from the individual General Occurrence Reports we can flesh out those categories (such as the 14-19 age group) which appear to suffer from a particular bias in police classification.

For example, many of the rape victims who were classified as "idle", "unemployed" or "on welfare" were very young women. They were also classified as single women. In general, the young women most likely to have their cases classified as unfounded were those young women who were *not* living at home and were, in some sense, "independent" of their parents, but who had no occupational skills. On the General Occurrence Reports, they were frequently classified as "hippies", "incorrigible", "unmanageable" or "promiscuous"; some had already come to the attention of other social agencies such as the Children's Aid Society or the Juvenile Court. Thus, the young woman who is not under parental control, is in a very vulnerable position. She is liable to be raped because of her age, but she is unlikely to be regarded as a "credible" complainant because she has forsaken parental protection. If she has engaged in sexual relationships and has failed to find her way into an acceptable female occupation, her situation is even worse.

From the point of view of the criminal justice system, some of the most difficult cases are those involving young victims who are either living apart from their parents or who engage in a great deal of friction while living with them, who do not attend school regularly, and who do not have acceptable job skills. These are the cases that are weeded out most successfully at the level of police involvement, and at later stages of the judicial process. Of the cases which proceeded to preliminary hearing in Ontario, Clark, Barr-Carley and Ward found that 71.4% of the victims involved were between the ages of 14 and 24, with 39.3% between the ages of 14 and 19; 62.5% were single, but of these, 36.7% were in fact dependent female children living at home with their parents. *None* of these cases involved women classified as "unemployed", "idle" or "on welfare". The largest single occupational category for victims whose cases proceed to preliminary hearing was that of "student", accounting for fully 43.4% of all such cases, but only 20.0% of the founded cases in our study involved students. This shows, then, a further refinement in the filtering process between the level of police involvement and the decision to proceed further in the judicial system. Cases which the court selects to go forward are those in which the victim is young, living at home, and in regular attendance at school. The most "credible" rape victims are in fact dependent children of solidly middle-class families; they have not deviated from the norms expected of them. But that the whole judicial system displays a clear bias against women who do not conform to this picture of respectability is clearly demonstrated by the data.

Similarly, a combination of value judgments appears to account for the discrimination against women in the 30-34 age group. In our study, only 1 out of the 6 cases in this category was classified as founded. Of the 4 victims who were described as "separated", 1 was "on welfare", and 1 was a cleaner; another's occupation was described as "nil". The only "single" woman in this category was listed by the police as a "mental patient". It is obvious that rape victims of low economic status and dubious social reputation are not regarded as "credible" witnesses by the judicial system, and are not granted their rights of redress under the law.

alcohol use

Though the victim's age, occupation and marital status may be the most critical determinants of police classification, her condition when she first reports the offence to the police will also affect its ultimate classification. One of the clearest patterns around a single variable was that involving the victim's use of alcohol. There was a 100.0% correlation between an "unfounded" classification and the victim's description on the General Occurrence Report as "drunk" or "intoxicated". (See table 11.)

It is important to distinguish, however, between the victim's actual use of alcohol, and police perceptions of that use. Table 11 indicates police perceptions of the victim, as it summarizes police comments on her condition at the time of first report; when the police perceived rape victims to be "drunk", they consistently classified their cases as unfounded. Table 5, on the other hand   (see page 69), indicates the use of alcohol in the rape situation as reported by the victim herself; this table shows that the victim's consumption of alcohol did not always interfere with the classification of her report as founded. In other words, what is important to police classification is not whether the victim had been drinking, but whether the first impression of the investigating police officer was that she was drunk.

It should be repeated, however, that this correlation may not reflect any disbelief on the part of the police that an offence occurred. Cases involving drunk or intoxicated victims make notoriously bad cases from the prosecution's point of view, and in labelling such cases as "unfounded", the police may simply be screening out cases which are unlikely to lead to a satisfactory outcome at trial. But there is no reason to assume that police officers are any more free of prejudice than jurors. It may well be that they share general beliefs that drunk women are fair game, that drunk women deserve what they get, or, at least, that drunk women are more likely to have been responsible for

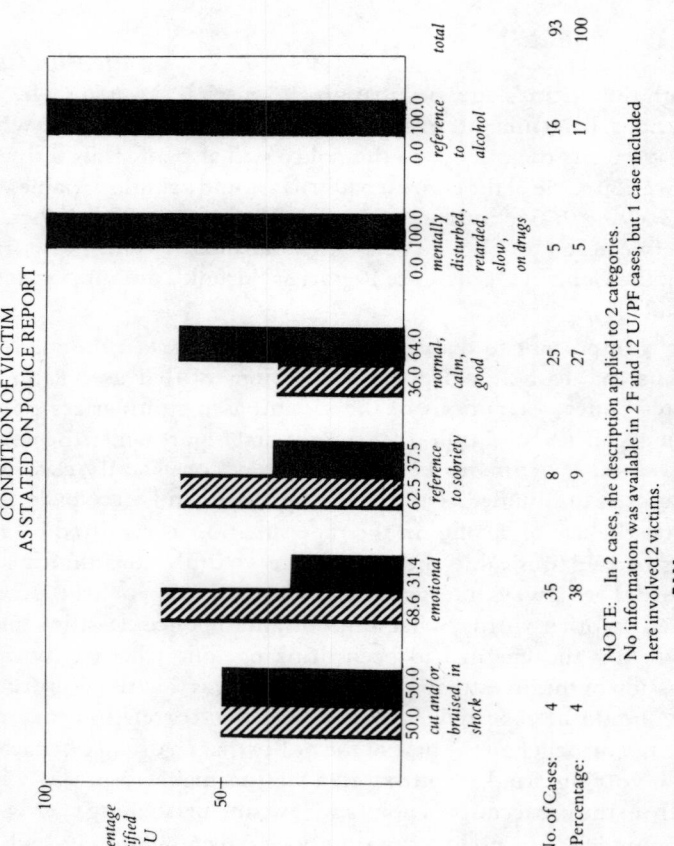

TABLE 11
CONDITION OF VICTIM
AS STATED ON POLICE REPORT

NOTE: In 2 cases, the description applied to 2 categories.
No information was available in 2 F and 12 U/PF cases, but 1 case included
here involved 2 victims.

percentage classified as founded
percentage classified as unfounded by the police,
and as unfounded/possibly founded by Clark/Lewis

the rape. Drinking, especially to "excess", is still not considered a suitable activity for women. While some of the "unfounded" classifications in these cases may have been dictated by the practical realities of prosecution, it is unlikely that all were. If the police judgment is, in effect, that the case will be difficult to prosecute, then this should be made clear in the report. If the victim's use of alcohol means that she has an unclear memory of the rape, then her use of alcohol is relevant to the disposition of her case, but if she can give a clear, consistent and coherent account of the event, the fact that she may have been drinking should be considered irrelevant.

On the other hand, the police can hardly be faulted for screening out cases which will involve a needless expenditure of public time and money, and the legal system as a whole is surely to be criticized if it forces police officers to classify cases as unfounded merely because the victim's use of alcohol will prejudice a jury against her. It is up to the Crown to confront such prejudice directly. That such prejudice is likely shared by crown attorneys is no doubt true as well, but the theory of adversarial justice which demands that defence lawyers provide the best case possible for the defendant, no matter what the cost to the victim, and no matter what their own beliefs, also demands that crown prosecutors make the best case possible for the Crown, no matter what their beliefs about the morality of the witness, and no matter what prejudices they may meet on the part of jurors.

victim's "mental state"

There are two other factors which may be influential in shaping police classification and both are, again, considerations which have a bearing on the ultimate outcome at trial. In a small number of cases (3), the victim's "mental state" was given as the reason for not continuing the case. (See table 11.) In 2 of these cases, the victim had a history of past mental illness, and in the other she was under psychiatric care at the time of her report. In all 3 cases, nothing but the victim's mental state was given as justification for a U classification. The psychiatrist of one woman who was receiving treatment did not believe that she had been raped, though no reason for this belief was given in the police report. These cases seem to present problems similar to those surrounding very young victims. The complainant is regarded as a dependent child, who is not responsible for her actions.

Many people, both women and men, voluntarily seek psychiatric help for what they believe to be their problems, and it would obviously be grossly unfair to consider such persons as suffering from a mental disorder which impaired their credibility. Similarly, a history of mental illness should not be a reason for disbelieving rape victims. The legal system should not endorse a policy which leaves female mental patients open to be raped with impunity. If women are genuinely suffering from mental illness then they deserve more rather than less protection from the law; if they have sought, or are currently seeking psychiatric assistance, there is no reason to assume that they are less credible than other rape victims.

One case underlined the injustice of the present system very poignantly and sharply. It involved a young woman who was grossly retarded; though she was twenty-one years old, she had a mental age of eight. This woman was abducted from a public fairground and taken to a motel, where she was sexually assaulted. Medical evidence corroborated the fact that penetration had taken place, and it was proved that the woman had had no other occasion to engage in sexual intercourse. The problem which arose in classification was the question of whether such a person could *consent* at all, and the question is a legitimate one. However, it is no justification for classifying such a case as unfounded; this is simply to say to the potential rapist, "Pick a retarded victim and you can do what you like." Cases like this one should be treated under other sections of the Criminal Code, or new legal principles should be developed to deal with them.[10] Why not apply the civil assault rule that you take your victim as you find her?[11] The victim's inability to give that full, voluntary consent which we consider necessary for consensual sexual relations should not be a reason for letting the offender escape punishment, but for punishing him more severely. Women of this kind need more protection than others, and our legal processes should reflect that fact.

time of first report

Another factor which affects classification is the interval of time between the rape and the victim's report of it. Police expect the victim to report the crime at the first available opportunity, and her failure to do so casts doubt upon her credibility. While there may be some psychological truth to the belief that a woman who is raped is likely to report it to someone fairly soon after the attack, it is hardly a truth so universal that her failure to report it at the very first available opportunity should be taken as discrediting her story. The theory of first report assumes that most women will be so upset by rape, literally verging on the hysterical, that they will in fact be unable *not* to report it to the first person they see afterwards. But that assumption is clearly open to question. Not everyone responds to stress with hysteria, and not everyone who is raped should be hysterical. The expectation that women will react this way reflects nothing other than a general belief that most women identify rape as the worst thing that can happen to them, an event which is tantamount to instant mental breakdown.

Many women recognize that, bad as rape is, it is not as terrible as being seriously injured or killed. Moreover, people have different ways of expressing distress, ways which are as much a product of social conditioning as of individual temperament. Many women prefer to wait until they are with those they trust before expressing their true feelings about the rape; and given that rape is still treated as a "shameful" act, it is hardly surprising that some victims choose not to discuss it with a chance passer-by.

In the present study, 1 case was classified as unfounded because the victim did not report the rape to the first person she met, who happened to be a taxi driver; she waited to tell her boyfriend a short time later. This seems to indicate an undue reliance on the rule of first report, rather than on the spirit which should underlie it. No woman should be denied the redress of the law simply because she happens to be somewhat more in control of her emotions, or less able to express them to strangers, than other women. If her failure to report to the first available person can be adequately explained, it should not detract from her credibility.

women who "can't be raped"

We have now examined in detail the victim-related variables determining police classification of rape reports. The police process of classification is intended to filter out all cases in which an offence did not occur, and all cases which look particularly difficult to prosecute. But as we remarked at the beginning of this chapter, all of the major factors which make a case a "bad" one, are directly linked to the victim. To a very large extent, it is the character of the reporting rape victim which determines whether or not a reported offence will be classified as founded, and passed on in the judicial system. This process of selection may have nothing to do with whether or not the complainant was actually raped. In effect, the law is saying that some women can be raped and some women can't, and it is instructive to summarize the features of those women whose cases are by and large classified as unfounded.

The rape victim whose case does not make it past the first stage of the criminal justice system may be perceived as "drunk" when she is first interviewed by the police. She may be a teenager, who does not live at home, has a record of "unmanageable" behaviour, or has already come to the attention of school authorities, the Children's Aid Society, or the Juvenile Court. She may be between thirty and forty years of age, and either separated, divorced, or living in a common-law relationship. Regardless of her age, she may be "idle", unemployed, or on welfare. She may also have been under previous psychiatric care; she probably wasn't hysterical when she reported the crime; she may not have reported the offence to the first possible person following its commission. And, as we have discussed in the chapter on "The Crime", she may have "known" the offender, she may have voluntarily accompanied her assailant to his residence and been raped there, or she may have voluntarily accepted a ride in his car.

Women who display a number of these features will not have their sexual assault defined as rape. They quite literally cannot be raped, because "rape" is a social and legal definition, and these are not the sort of women that society believes *can* be raped. It is virtually impossible for these women to complain of rape and have their complaint taken seriously. Their vulnerable position in society—itself a function of age, lack of occupational skills, and, in general, low socio-economic status—leaves them open to rape with very little hope of redress.

A number of women in our study whose cases were classified as unfounded were notified that they could, if they wished, swear out a warrant with a Justice of the Peace and proceed on their own. Understandably, no women were willing to take this course of action. These women must not only endure social and economic oppression; they must also sustain physical and sexual abuse without either legal redress or emotional support. As the following examples show, these women are easily victimized.

One case involved a woman whom the police described as being on welfare, and having a history of mental illness.[12] She had been separated from her husband for seven years, and had borne an "illegiti-mate" child since that time. Despite strong medical and material evi-dence that she had been raped, her report was later classified as un-founded, largely because she had a history of drinking, and because she was unwilling to co-operate further in the investigation. Her un-willingness to co-operate was hardly surprising in the light of her past; people who have had previous dealings with public institutions are often justifiably reluctant to have any more contact with "profes-sionals" than is absolutely necessary. Moreover, it is likely that this victim knew how little chance her case had of reaching successful pro-secution. It was also clear, through interviews which the police con-ducted with her landlord and with the godfather of her child, that at least some of her associates did not believe her story. They described her as a habitual drunk, given to "shacking up with coloureds".

This woman displayed many of the characteristics which appear to lead to an "unfounded" classification. She was a single parent, on welfare, and had undergone psychiatric care, albeit for a short period of time. She had a reputation (whether founded or not) for "exces-sive" drinking and for unacceptable sexual behaviour. The facts of her case strongly support her contention that she was raped; nevertheless, she was not believed. It is not difficult to imagine a different response had she been a middle-class married woman with a "good" reputation in the community; she would certainly have received (at least overtly) a more sympathetic response from friends, relatives, and public in-stitutions.

Another case involved a twenty-year-old student from Quebec. She was a visitor to Toronto, and while in the Yorkville area met a man with whom she spent some time during the evening. He told her that he had an extra bed in his home, and would allow her to sleep there if she wished. She agreed, returned to his home and went to sleep (fully clothed) on the spare bed. Just as she was falling asleep, however, she was awakened to find the man fondling her breasts and kissing her. She began to cry and shout, but was overcome by her attacker. After the rape, she went to the other bed and slept. She then left and reported the rape to her boyfriend, but "he didn't take me seriously and started to laugh". She later complained to her mother, who had met her in Toronto, and subsequently reported the rape.

This victim was able to identify her assailant's home, and the man was interviewed by the police. He admitted having sexual intercourse with the victim, but denied raping her, saying he hadn't used "any more force than is usual for males during the preliminaries". Thereupon, the police classified the complaint as unfounded, assuming that the victim had been encouraged to report rape by her mother. It seems implausible that she would have told her mother she had been raped if she had not. It is quite understandable, on the other hand, that she would at first hesitate to report rape, in the face of her boyfriend's disbelief, but that she would later be able to do so after receiving some support from her mother.

The victim in this case effectively abdicated her right to legal redress by transgressing established norms of "acceptable" female behaviour. Though it may have been unwise for her to accept accommodation from a man she didn't know well, this should not have given him the right to rape her. The concept that some women are "fair game", however, is one which is shared by the police, the courts, and society at large. This is a conclusion which can be substantiated by other studies of rape as well. Mohr's work,[13] for example, reveals a similar pattern in the disposition of rape cases. Those cases in which the victim had been drinking, had accepted a ride from a stranger, or had displayed otherwise "disreputable" behaviour, were usually terminated by the withdrawal or dismissal of the charge, or by a "not guilty" verdict. Those cases which led to a "guilty" verdict, on the other hand, often involved more "respectable" victims: a married woman whose husband was at work was threatened with harm to her small child; a young girl who had accepted a ride had been a virgin prior to the rape, and had known one of the car's occupants. Men who rape such women are less likely to escape punishment than those who choose less worthy targets. But men who assault the women that society does not care to protect can usually avoid the penalties of the law.

6
the rapist

One of the greatest difficulties with rape research is the lack of data on the rapist, who is, after all, the perpetrator of the offence. The majority of rapists escape notice altogether, because most rape goes unreported, and when a victim does report the crime her account is bound to be somewhat impressionistic if her assailant is unknown to her. Records of Arrest are more reliable sources of information, but it should be remembered that the police will search for a suspect only if a case has been classified as "founded". And studies of convicted rapists, which provide our most complete picture of the rape offender, also reflect the biases of a judicial system which brings only some rape cases to court and some rape offenders to conviction. However, the problem of rape can never be understood without an analysis of the rape offender and his motivations. For this reason, we decided to examine closely all the information available to us, despite its limitations.

Twenty-five out of the 42 "founded" cases in our study had been cleared by arrest, and the Records of Arrest for these cases provided us with some data on 32 offenders. (One case was a pair-rape, and another involved 6 offenders.) We also studied any information supplied by rape victims on the General Occurrence Reports, for all 104 cases in our data base. This information reflected the victim's subjective view of her rapist, and was clearly less reliable than that appearing on the Record of Arrest form, but in many instances it was also the only information available to us. The Records of Arrest contained very little descriptive data, giving only the offender's age, occupation and place of birth. General Occurrence Reports varied a great deal in the kind of information they contained, but were a rich fund of descriptive detail concerning the event, the offender, and any conversation that had taken place.

place of birth, age and physical appearance

The first picture to emerge from the data is that of a fairly average Canadian male, someone who could be the man-next-door. The vast majority of arrested rapists were white (71.9%) and Canadian-born (63.4%).[1] (See tables 12 and 13). This certainly disproves any "outside elements" theory of rape; Toronto's rape problem is genuinely its own.

Like McCaldon and Ringrose,[2] we found that "rapists are generally young men, only slightly older than their victims". Slightly over 40% were over 30 years of age, with almost an additional 40% between the ages of 25 and 29.[3] (See table 14.) In a random sample of 50 offenders from our study, we computed specific victim-offender age correlations and found that there was an age difference of not more than 9 years in almost half (48.0%) of these cases. This is similar to Mohr's finding, that "in terms of age differences, most cases (77.2%) fall within a range of ten years".[4] Though rapists tended, over-all, to be slightly older than their victims, it is clear that women of any age are vulnerable to attack, and that their assailants may be as much as 15 to 25 years their junior.

In weight and height, the rapists in our study appeared to represent both the range and average for Canadian men in general. At the same time, they clearly fell short of the "he-man" ideal of television advertising and *Playboy* magazine. Some descriptive information was available on 50 offenders, who had been involved in 38 of the 104 cases in our data base. Information on height (available for 31 offenders) described them as being from under 5'5" to over 6'0", with an average height of approximately 5'9". Information on weight (available for 24 offenders) described them as being from 130 lbs. to over 200 lbs., and a further 23 offenders were described in general terms as being of "slight", "slim" or "medium" build. Thus, the typical rapist is 5'9" or less, and of slight to medium build. Though he is not conspicuously different from other men, in height and weight, he appears to be a bit smaller than average. This is surprising, as one would expect a rape victim to remember her assailant as being somewhat larger than he actually was.

Data on hair length, available for 25 offenders, showed that 64% had short hair, 24% had medium-length hair, and 12% had long hair. Some rapists were dressed in suits and ties (20%), others in casual clothing such as sports jackets and trousers (20%), and some (a further 20%) seemed to fit the popular stereotype of a "greaser"—lots of tattoos, body odour, and unkempt, dirty hair. Little data was available on the remaining 40%, but on the whole they were "clean", "neat" and beardless, conforming to the basically "straight" image of the Canadian male.

TABLE 12
OFFENDERS' RACIAL ORIGIN

Racial Origin	Number	Percentage
White	23	71.9
Black	6	18.8
Oriental	1	3.1
Canadian Indian	2	6.3
TOTAL	32	100.1

TABLE 13
OFFENDERS' PLACE OF BIRTH

Birth Place	Number	Percentage
Ontario	8	26.7
Other Canada	5	16.7
Canada (not specified)	6	20.0
United States	4	13.3
Europe	5	16.7
Jamaica	1	3.3
Japan	1	3.3
TOTAL	30	100.0

NOTE: No information was available in 2 cases.

TABLE 14
OFFENDERS' AGE

Age Group	Number	Percentage
Under 15	0	0.0
15-19	2	6.3
20-24	5	15.6
25-29	12	37.5
30-34	4	12.5
35-39	1	3.1
40-44	6	18.8
over 44	2	6.3
TOTAL	32	100.1

Up to this point, there is little to distinguish rapists from most Canadian men. Judging from the comments made by their victims, however, rapists are not an especially handsome lot. They were described on General Occurrence Reports in the following ways: "definitely large bulging blue eyes"; "tobacco-stained teeth...running at an angle, slightly overlapping one another"; "thin face and lips"; "very fat lips"; "balding, bags under eyes, very pale, looked sick"; "small-appearing eyes, possibly from use of alcohol"; "prominent nose"; "high forehead"; "very pointed and large nose". While one would expect rape victims to find their assailants unattractive, it may be significant that negative statements about the rapist's appearance were made in fully 24% of the cases studied.

occupation

Among the most interesting data, however, is that which describes the occupation of the offender. (See table 15.) Almost without exception, the rapists in our study came from lower socio-economic groups. Approximately one quarter (24.1%) were classified as "idle" or "unemployed", and only 1 was a student. Another 24.1% were described as "truck drivers", 13.8% were described as "labourers", and 6.9% were described as "clerks". Semi-skilled workers, including a service-station attendant, baker's helper and metal cutter, accounted for 20.7% of the offenders; skilled workers, including an optical grinder and a barber, accounted for only 6.9%. Only 3.4% or 1 offender was described as "self-employed"; he was a landlord. Mohr also found that a majority of offenders (75%) were of low socio-economic status. In addition, he found that 9.4% were semi-skilled, 12.5% were skilled, and 3.1% were students.[5] McCaldon does not give the employment background of the offenders which he studied, but classifies them only according to "socio-economic status—upper, middle, lower". Within these classifications, however, 0% of the rapists in his study were "upper", 59% were "middle", and 41% were "lower".[6] His study appears to show more rapists within the middle-class range than either ours or Mohr's, but as McCaldon himself remarks,

> ...these ratings were made by penitentiary officers, who tended to categorize offenders as "middle" so long as they were above the bare subsistence level. Rapists are mainly from the lower socio-economic groups.[7]

TABLE 15
OFFENDERS' OCCUPATION

Occupation	Number	Percentage
"Idle" or unemployed	7	24.1
Truck driver	7	24.1
Labourer	4	13.8
Clerk	2	6.9
Semi-skilled	6	20.7
Skilled	2	6.9
Self-employed	1	3.4
TOTAL	29	99.9

NOTE: No information was available in 3 cases.

Other studies have also found that most arrested rapists are from the lower socio-economic strata.[8] The obvious inference, of course, is that men from these strata are more likely to commit rape than other men, but it seems to us that this conclusion should be approached with caution. To begin with, a suspect can be arrested only if a rape case has been classified as founded. This founded classification means that some pre-selection of rape reports has already taken place; it may indicate a variety of judgments about the victim, her attacker, and their social status in relation to one another. If the rapist is better placed in the social hierarchy than the alleged victim, it may not seem credible that he would have to, or want to, rape her. If the reverse is true, especially if the victim is a "respectable" witness, it will appear much more believable that the offender would have to resort to physical violence to achieve his purpose. Generally, suspects from lower socio-economic groups are more likely to be perceived by a jury and officers of the Court as the sort of men likely to have committed rape, and therefore, they are more likely to be convicted and labelled as "rapists". At all levels of the judicial process, they will be perceived as the sort of men who would resort to the use or threat of physical violence to get what they want.

We also know, on the basis of work done with the Toronto Rape Crisis Centre, that many unreported rape cases involve men who are from higher socio-economic groups than the men who turn up on arrest warrants. These cases may involve landlords, employers, or professionals with private offices. Usually (though not necessarily), the women involved are not as well placed as the men, and they may be in an openly exploitable situation. Such cases rarely come to the attention of the police.

The selective filtering of rape cases through the judicial system clearly reveals a bias against men of low socio-economic status. Such men are often convicted as much for that status as for the crime of rape. This is not to deny the obvious fact that men from low socio-economic backgrounds are more likely to commit rape than other men, or at least, are more likely to commit the kind of rape offence which is reported to the police and classified as founded. But their class does provide us with another approach to this whole question. Men who fit the profile of the arrested rape suspect have little real status in our society. They are neither rich nor powerful, and it is possible that they commit rape largely because they have no other means of gaining access to the women they want. The extent to which rape is a function of a dead-end class position has, we feel, been greatly underestimated,[9] and we will return to this question in a later chapter of this book.

awareness of guilt

But if most arrested rapists are basically average men, set apart only by their low socio-economic status and perhaps by their lack of physical attractiveness, why do they rape, and how do they perceive their actions? We studied the General Occurrence Reports for any information concerning the rapist's personal background, attitudes towards women, and perceptions of himself. Twenty-two of these reports described conversations which took place between the victim and the offender during the commission of the offence. These conversations were extremely valuable in helping us to assess the rapist's motivation and state of mind.

Very early in our research, we were struck by the fact that the majority of rapists involved in these cases did not believe that they had done anything wrong. They did not see their behaviour as different from other men's, and resisted admitting that they had broken the law. Some of them went to quite incredible lengths to see their behaviour as "normal" and "acceptable". What emerges from an analysis of these cases is a continuum of attitudes and behaviour among rape offenders. At one end of the continuum is the man who makes no attempt to disguise his behaviour, but does not see it as wrong because he does not believe that his victim's wishes are of any relevance whatever. Rape is a meaningless concept for him, because he does not see women as self-determining individuals. At the other end of the continuum is the rapist who will try to avoid seeing his actions as rape. He recognizes that his victim has (at least theoretically) the right to refuse inter-course, and will therefore attempt to deny the coerciveness of the act and to characterize it, instead, as a "date" or a "seduction".

One example of the former extreme is a man who raped one of his employees. After the rape she struggled away, shouting angry insults at him, but his reaction was merely to laugh at her. He was so sure of himself that he made no attempt to intimidate the victim or to avoid detection. In fact, the victim did lay a complaint and the police arrested him soon afterwards at his home. He was thoroughly unconcerned; no doubt he had been indulging in such behaviour for years and none of his previous victims had thought it worth while having him arrested. Another rapist dragged his victim to the floor, saying, "You don't want to fuck but you are going to fuck, you son of a bitch." In still another case, the victim met her assailant at a party and accepted a ride from him:

> When the victim told the suspect to keep his hands to himself the offender slapped her across the face several times and called her a bitch and a slut....When the offender put his penis in her, "I told him I was menstruating and he said that was all right that I was only a pig anyway".

These offenders recognize their victims' hostility and resistance, but are not perturbed by it. The victim's feelings are irrelevant because, to this type of rapist, she is not an autonomous person whose wishes should be respected; she is simply an object to gratify his wishes.

More commonly, however, the offender tries to see the situation in more generally acceptable terms. One man who attacked a hitch-hiker asked for his victim's telephone number after the rape was completed and promised to pay her $500.00 if she would "sleep with him" again. In another hitch-hiking case, the offender took down the address of his victim, drove her home, shook her hand, and said goodbye as he drove off into the night. In another case, the rapist remarked to his victim (while standing over her with a knife), "This is my lucky night. I was trying doors and found yours open."

Protestations of love are quite common. In one case, a woman of forty-four was asleep in her bedroom when attacked by a stranger fifteen years her junior:

> During the struggle the assailant stated that he loved her....All the time that he was trying this he kept saying to her that he loved her very much.

Another rapist, who attacked his victim in a heavily wooded area,

> ...fondled the victim's breasts and tried to kiss her, asking her if she loved him....This man shouted "goodbye" as he ran off when he was finished.

One rapist established an atmosphere of extreme violence and then proceeded as if the situation were one between new lovers, where indeed, the woman was a virgin. First,

> He informed the victim that he had done this many times before, and no harm would come to her if she cooperated. "There was only one woman that resisted and I broke her neck" he told me.

And then, "I am only going to make love to you, not hurt you," he said. In this case, the offender wished the victim to engage in what would, in a non-coercive situation, be quite usual and acceptable forms of foreplay, including fondling and kissing his penis. Following this,

> "He told me that he would be very gentle with me." When she refused to insert his penis into her vagina, "he then sunk his teeth into the fleshy part of the upper left breast, cutting the skin and leaving teeth marks." With this, she complied, and on complaining that it hurt her, "he then asked me, 'Do you want me to go all the way?'"

Frequently, the offender wanted the victim to participate pretty actively in his fantasy. It was very common for a rapist to ask his victim whether or not she was enjoying the situation, and to demand a positive response. This type of demand was reported in 6 cases in our study, and in 1 case, the man

> ...undid his pants and pulled them down enough to expose himself and got on top of the victim and inserted his penis in the victim's vagina and said, "Do you like it?"...She did not reply. He then asked again in a louder voice, "Do you like it?" Again the victim did not reply. He then asked in a very fierce voice, "Do you like it?" and then pushed on the victim's shoulders. At this time she repeated "Yes".

As soon as this victim made the requisite "admission", her assailant ejaculated. In another case, the offender wanted the victim to assure him that his penis was bigger than her husband's. And in still another, the offender carried on a virtual running patter.

This kind of rapist will pretend to himself that the situation is "normal". He tries to see the victim as someone he loves, and perhaps as someone who loves him. He expects the usual preliminary gestures of kissing and fondling, and wants to be assured that he is a good performer. Afterwards, he wants a normal parting: idle chit-chat, a cigarette or two, an exchange of telephone numbers, and a friendly goodbye. He often uses only enough violence to perpetrate the rape, and will try to downplay it as much as possible. He uses the threat or reality of violence to set the stage, but then will pretend that the violence does not exist, and will proceed as if the rape were a perfectly normal encounter with a consenting female. At the outer limit, he sees it as seduction rather than rape.

Between the two extremes—the man who is unconcernedly and frankly coercive, and the man who must deceive himself that his actions are not rape—there are many other offenders who make only an erratic attempt to disguise the coercive nature of their behaviour. One rapist, who abducted his victim off the street, made some effort to normalize the situation but repeatedly impressed upon the victim that she was in very real danger:

> He raped her in his car, following which he put his hand over her mouth and then placed his other hand on her throat and said he was going to kill her....He then dragged her, nude, out of the car to a grassy area about 50 ft. away where he had the victim sit nude on the wet grass. He got her clothes and told her to sit and talk, asked her to light him a cigarette which she did. He talked about being married, having a wife and six kids. He then raped her again by placing his hands on her throat and threatening her with death.

This type of offender appears to recognize the reality of violence as an element in his behaviour, and even to take satisfaction in the power which it gives him over his victim. At the same time, he will attempt to obscure or ignore the coerciveness of the situation, because he does not want to see himself as the sort of man who must rely on force to get what he wants.

Other rapists display a complicated mixture of deception, self-deception and rationalization. In one case:

> The suspect never stopped talking. His wife was a nurse, that he had been a homosexual at age 12-14 years, that this was the sixth time he had done this, that the first time had been to a young woman in a suburban area....He had received a "dose" from this woman. He had never beaten anyone to the point of submission, asked if she was a virgin, asked her name and address, asked her if she had trouble reaching a climax. He stated that he didn't drink, didn't smoke, and didn't hang around bars. This was going to be his last time, that he knew he was a pathetic case, that a hospital couldn't help him, that his relations with his wife had been better lately, and that this would be the last time he would have to do this....The suspect stated that he was emotionally disturbed, also that the victim would be crushed emotionally, that he wanted to keep a good relationship with his mother-in-law. When he let the victim out of his auto, he said he never did have a knife, and that he was sorry he raped her.

This offender had abducted his victim from the parking lot of a large downtown Toronto motor-hotel, at 2:00 in the afternoon, despite his victim's resistance and the attempts of several witnesses to stop him. He bound and gagged the victim, and kept her literally underfoot under the front seat of his car until he had driven well out into the country. He used considerable violence on his victim and this was not, in fact, his "last time". This man was apprehended later in 1970 after committing two more rapes, one of which exhibited a rather high degree of violence. On arrest, he was charged with six counts of rape, two counts of attempted rape, and one count of assault causing bodily harm. Some of the details which this man had given this particular victim about himself were then found to be untrue. No doubt a number of his false statements were the product of self-deception, but some of them appeared to be deliberate attempts to mislead his victim—either to make detection difficult, or to elicit the victim's sympathy and cooperation. In such situations, of course, success in gaining the victim's co-operation only strengthens the offender's belief that he is seducing rather than raping the victim.

Only five rapists in our study showed any awareness of guilt, and four of these tried to deny responsibility for their actions by blaming it on other causes—prison, a bad marriage, an unhappy childhood. The fifth had the simplest of all explanations for behaviour which he clearly believed to be wrong. This was a group rape:

> He didn't want to do it, but if he didn't, the others would "beat the shit out of him"....They talked of having done this to other women.

In general, however, most of the rapists we studied did not show any awareness of guilt. They either did not feel rape to be morally wrong, or they glossed over the true nature of their behaviour in a more or less consistent attempt to characterize it as "normal".

Other researchers have not commented upon the rapist's attempts at normalization, but many studies describe incidents and behaviour that could be interpreted in this way. MacDonald mentions that many offenders demand co-operation and affection from their victims,[10] and comments that "touching solicitude may be shown for the victim's welfare".[11] He discusses one particularly revealing conversational exchange which clearly illustrates the rapist's unwillingness to recognize that he is doing anything wrong:

> A victim asked her assailant, "Is that always the way you have to get a girl, by rape?" He became very angry, saying, "Did I rape you?" reaching for his knife and adding, "In that case, I'll have to kill you." The girl quickly told him that he did not rape her.[12]

MacDonald also comments that many rapists express remorse for their crime; for example, "A grateful offender paid a florist to send roses to his victim".[13] This is an ambiguous gesture at best. It seems to us that the expression of remorse must necessarily involve some recognition of wrongdoing, and sending roses is certainly not a clear-cut illustration of this. It is the sort of action one would expect from a man who feels pleased with himself at having accomplished a seduction, and not from someone who feels sorry about having raped a woman.

McCaldon, in his attempt to assess the rapist's attitude to the crime, found that the offender "admits" his offence in 33% of the cases, "denies" it in 27% and "rationalizes" it in 33%. He comments that "rapists...have a tendency to avoid a full admission of guilt with an appropriately contrite attitude. Instead, in two-thirds of the cases, one hears—'I'm here on a phoney beef'...or 'So I might have been a little rough, but she was asking for it,' or 'I might have done it, but I was too drunk to remember'."[14] His conclusions certainly support our contention that most rapists do not see their behaviour as morally wrong. Glueck's study of rapists also presents similar data.[15]

aggression and hostility

Though many offenders used only the degree of violence needed to accomplish the rape, a number used more than was necessary, even while attempting to normalize the situation. Again, the rapists in our study displayed a range of behaviour. Some of the offenders showed extraordinary callousness towards their victims, engaging in both verbal and physical abuse. Others used more violence than the situation demanded, but at the same time tried to engage in "normal" conversation and other unexceptional behaviour.

We believe that these variations correspond to the offender's identification of "masculinity" with sexual aggression. Some rapists appear to believe that, in order to live up to their own image of manliness, they must manifest hostility towards their victims and demonstrate real power over them. They must make their victims fear and perhaps even dislike them. To such men, women are not people; they are simply pieces of meat. Other rapists appear to identify masculinity and aggression less strongly; they seem to want both the sense of power which violence creates, and the reassurance that they don't need to rely on violence to achieve sexual contact. The rapist's conception of "masculine" behaviour may also vary according to the particular circumstances and the particular victim. These are possibilities that can only be verified by further research into the rapist's attitude towards his own sexuality, towards male and female sexuality in general, and towards the sexuality of particular women.

problems with orgasm and erection

While our data did not allow us to draw any definitive conclusions about the psychodynamics of rapists, they strongly suggested an image of the rapist as a socially inadequate person. While there is nothing remarkable about his appearance, he is certainly not handsome. He lacks power, money and prestige. He uses physical force to achieve sexual contact with women, but may go through elaborate mental manoeuvres to deny that this is so.

Once a picture of the rapist as "loser" started to emerge, we began to wonder if his sexual competence was also inadequate. No previous studies have considered whether or not the rapist had difficulty with orgasm or erection during the crime, though MacDonald mentions in passing that erection is sometimes a problem. He links it with the offender's demand for co-operation or affection, stating that "demands for affection take the form of requests for a loving response,"[16] but it seems more likely that some offenders have difficulty achieving erection unless they can believe that what they are engaged in is a seduction rather than a rape.

McCaldon attempted to assess what he calls "heterosexual adequacy", judging it to be "good" in 56% of the cases studied, "fair" in 33% and "poor" in 11%. His own comments about this assessment, however, are very interesting:

> This amounted to a rough guess in each case as to how well he managed in an adult heterosexual relationship. Comments about wives or girlfriends were most revealing and relied upon. This rating probably represents, not a high proportion of perfect adequacy amongst the rapists, but rather their reluctance to admit to sexual inadequacies, plus the apparent aggressive normality of their usual sexual behaviour.[17]

If rapists believe that a high degree of aggressiveness is necessary to demonstrate masculinity, then this will be characteristic of all their relationships and they may lack a sense of moral wrongdoing in what is in fact a rape situation. Of course, such men are not likely to admit any sort of sexual inadequacy.

In the present study, 5 out of the 22 offenders who had engaged in conversation with their victims referred to a wife or girlfriend. It was difficult to extract any information on sexual adequacy from the General Occurrence Reports, and only in the founded cases was there enough data to indicate any trends. (See table 16.) In the 42 founded cases, there was no reference to orgasm in 26 cases. In the remaining 16, there was an unqualified "yes" as to orgasm in only 3 cases. Orgasm was *not* achieved in 9 cases, and only with difficulty in 4. Thus, in fully a third of the founded cases, the offender encountered some difficulty in achieving orgasm. When we reviewed the General Occurrence Reports for these cases, we found that in 50% of the cases where difficulty with orgasm occurred, the offender's problem began with an inability to achieve a satisfactory erection. In the remaining 50%, the problem appeared to be restricted to difficulty achieving orgasm. Thus, a significant proportion of those who are labelled "rapists", and, in the popular mythology, have excessive sexual appetites, are incapable of achieving orgasm in the rape situation. There is, obviously, a certain amount of irony in this paradox.

Unfortunately, it is frequently a very bitter irony for the victim, because it is precisely in these situations that the victim's forcible

TABLE 16
ORGASM IN OFFENDER

Orgasm	Number	Percentage
Yes	3 *	7.0
No	9 *	20.9
Only with difficulty	4 *	10.2
No reference	26 *	61.9
TOTAL	42	100.0

*This group includes both offenders from a pair-rape.

NOTE: Only F cases were considered, as the data on U/PF cases was too incomplete for analysis.

confinement is prolonged and she is forced to suffer other sexual acts. In an attempt to achieve a satisfactory erection, or to reach orgasm when vaginal penetration fails, the offender may resort to anal intercourse, other sexual acts, the use of artificial lubricants, or to more bizarre acts (one rapist inserted a wooden bed leg into his victim's vagina). This is simply the rapist's desperate remedy for a desperate situation, but it sometimes results in far more serious harm and psychological shock to the victim than would otherwise be the case.

The data appears to confirm, therefore, that those men who are "losers" in many other respects are also losers in terms of their ability to maintain satisfactory sexual identities that do not depend on either the use or threat of physical force to create the conditions in which they can be sexually adequate, or on their rationalization of the rape situation as one of "love". We certainly do nothing for such men in convicting them, but we do nothing for women unless we convict them. And that is the ultimate irony with which we are left.

It is time, clearly, to devise new solutions. We cannot do that without understanding why our social structures have produced so many "losers" whose sexual alienation expresses itself in rape. In the next chapters of this book we will explore this question within the context of the historical changes that have defined the social relations between men and women. We will also outline the evolution of rape laws, analyzing their social purpose, and the values which they imply.

part 2
analysis and critique

7
women, property and rape

We began this book by probing the contradictions in public attitudes towards rape, contradictions which are also present in the theory and practice of the law. During the course of our study, we found ourselves confronted with further questions about the treatment and definition of rape in our society. The one clear and absolutely striking pattern revealed by our research, was the extent to which reported rapes are acknowledged to be "real" only if they involve certain types of victims. As the data clearly shows, the ultimate disposition of a rape report—whether or not it will lead to a charge and proceed to further phases of the criminal justice system—is determined almost entirely by the character and behaviour of the reporting rape victim. Nevertheless, it was clear to us, and is often, we believe, clear to the police as well, that rapes reported by women who do not conform to stereotypes of "respectability" are nonetheless genuine rapes. Obviously, some explanation of this contradiction is required. We need a theoretical framework which explains both the social causes of rape, and the social function of rape laws. Why does rape happen, and what purpose is served by rape laws which offer protection only to a restricted segment of the female population? It is our belief that the explanation for both of these questions lies in the history of women's status as a form of private property.

women as forms of private property

From its beginnings in Ancient Greece, western political and legal theory has rested on two main assumptions. The first is the assumption that individuals have a right to own private property and that inequality in the distribution of such property can be traced to natural differences between men. Thus, a fundamental cornerstone of western liberal democracy is the belief that private property and inequality in its distribution are justified. The second is the assumptions that men are naturally superior to women and that this inequality can be traced to natural differences between the sexes.[1] Thus, an equally fundamental cornerstone of western liberal democracy is the belief that legal, social and economic inequality between men and women is also justified. The first assumption laid the basis for a class society characterized by inequality between individuals and, ultimately, between classes of individuals. Those who held the greatest share of private wealth were held to be more "noble", "magnanimous", "just", or "wise", and later, more "rational" and "industrious" than those who did not own property. The second assumption laid the basis for a sexist society characterized by inequality between the sexes. The specific form that this inequality took made women the objects rather than the subjects of property rights: women were among the forms of private property owned and controlled by individual men. This inequality in the distribution of property rights was considered to be justified by differences between males and females. Those attributed with such rights were held to be stronger, more able, rational, and capable of realizing the loftier aspirations of the human spirit. Those denied such rights were held to be weaker, less able, emotional rather than rational, and incapable of rising above the demands of necessity imposed on them because of their unique capacity to bear children.

The law reflected these two assumptions, and institutionalized them within the social, legal and economic structure. The legal system confirmed, supported and perpetuated unequal relationships between individual men, and between sexes. Women simply were not considered to be "persons" under the law. They could not own property; they were denied access to the productive labour market; and, within marriage, they and their children were the property of their husbands. Their economic status was determined by that of their father or husband, and their unique status as women within this system was determined by their sexual and reproductive capacities.

An explanation of the origins of private property and of the nature and functioning of class society is a task well beyond the scope of this book. However, it is impossible to understand the problem of rape without understanding the historical evolution and development of the legal offence of rape, and it is impossible to do this without understanding the historical position of women. How is it, then, that women became forms of private property, and how did their transformation affect the development of laws against rape?

the origin of sexual and reproductive property

The emergence of a system of private property under individual ownership brought with it the need for a mechanism which could transfer accumulated private property from one generation to another. In order to keep assets intact across generations, determinate future individuals had to be identifiable as the future owners of those assets. Property was held by individual families, in which sole authority for the present and future disposition of property rested with the father. Families required offspring in order to preserve the family line, and preservation of lineage was itself necessary to keep family property intact over time. Since the father of the family was the legally entitled owner of its property, it was the father who needed an heir on whom to devolve the family assets, and the only available mechanism for determining future property rights was biological inheritance.

As is well known, a system of private property under individual ownership necessitated ownership of the means and products of production by the propertied classes. But as is much less well known or appreciated, it also required control of the means and products of *re*production, in order to ensure that there would be determinate heirs to function as the designatable future owners of individually-held accumulations of private property. Under this system of property distribution, in which property moved through family and blood lines, the primary function of the legal and social system was to provide adequate institutions and practices designed to preserve both blood lines and private property.

A system of biological inheritance could, however, work properly only if the family's biological heirs were clearly and certainly identifiable. And since the personality of the family was vested in the husband alone,[2] this meant that certainty of paternity was necessary if biological inheritance was to be an adequate institution for the preservation of family property across generations. Certainty of paternity was, therefore, a necessary feature of this system of property disposition, and certainty of paternity was possible only if the male property owner had exclusive access to one (or more) women. The husband had to be protected in his right of exclusive sexual access and in his right to control over the products of reproduction, and so he became the owner of his wife and children.

Ownership is simply the most efficient form of control. "Ownership" is nothing more than a set of legal rights and duties which ensures the most effective control over some form of property, whether it be a TV set, land holdings, stocks and bonds, or wives and children. Typically, this set of rights includes the right to exclusive use and disposition of the property in question, and it imposes a duty on others to return any property to the lawful owner which is his. The set of legal rights and duties articulating the structure of relations between the sexes, designed to ensure to male "heads of households" exclusive sexual access to the women they married and exclusive rights to the children they produced (but only, of course, where certainty of paternity was secure), amounted to a set of legal relations which gave the husbands property rights in the wife and children. Husbands had rights to their wives' sexual and reproductive capacities, were under no obligations to maintain any minimum standard of care for their families, and had an absolute right to dispose of any family property as they saw fit, regardless of the needs of their wives and children.[3] But wives, on their part, had a duty to obey and submit to their husbands, were legally prohibited from leaving them, and were liable to serious penalties for adultery. Children were also under an obligation to obey their father—at least until they reached the age of majority—and had no legal claim on family property independent of his will. Thus, the conversion of women and children into forms of private property resulted from the evolution of social and legal institutions designed to ensure effective control to men over the certainty of their future offspring, and thereby to fulfill the need for a settled principle of inheritance which could preserve property through time.

Marriage itself was one of the institutions designed to facilitate the transference of property.[4] Chief among the rights it gave to the husband was an absolute right to exclusive sexual access to his wife, and an absolute right to exclusive disposition of family property. It denied the wife any right to sexual or reproductive autonomy *vis-a-vis* her husband; it also denied her any right to share in the ownership (and hence, control and future disposition) of family property, regardless of the fact that she may well have made, and almost certainly did make, as much of a contribution to any increase in these holdings as he did.[5] The husband's rights with regard to his wife and the family property, together with her lack of rights with respect to family property and her duties to her husband, articulated a legal state between them in which the wife was a form of private property exclusively under the ownership and control of her husband. And husbands were expected to exercise both authority and control, frequently being penalized when or if they failed to do so.[6]

Thus it was that women became forms of private property. And thus it was too that the sexual and reproductive capacities of women became the sole qualities which gave women value. The function of a wife was to have babies and to provide another pair of hands for work that had to be done.[7] A barren wife was worthless, but a woman who could produce an heir was guaranteed a certain amount of security and respect. Even today, many women feel that they have an obligation to provide their husbands with a son; this accomplishment both validates their existence and solidifies their status as "good wives".

rape as an offence against property

Parallel to marriage law, rape law developed as another form of social control designed to regulate the orderly transfer of property. Under Anglo-Saxon law, rape, along with most other offences, was punished by orders to pay compensation and reparation. If a woman was raped, a sum was paid to either her husband or father, depending on who still exercised rights of ownership over her, and the exact amount of compensation depended on the woman's economic position and her desirability as an object of an exclusive sexual relationship. The sum was not paid to the woman herself; it was paid to her father or husband because he was the person who was regarded as having been wronged by the act.

Rape is simply theft of sexual property under the ownership of someone other than the rapist. When women are forms of private property, owned by fathers or husbands, with a value determined by their sexual and reproductive capacities, rape is an act of theft and trespass against the legal owner of the sexual property (that is, the woman) in question. In having intercourse with a woman who does not belong to him, a man is guilty of trespassing on the property of whoever does own her, and of stealing access to female sexuality to which he has no legal right. From the beginning, rape was perceived as an offence against property, not as an offence against the person on whom the act was perpetrated, and it has not lost the shrouds of these historical origins.

The fact that rape was originally perceived as an offence against one form of property owned by men, and that it has developed historically and legally within this conceptual framework, had several important consequences. First, just as with any other property offence, the punishment had to fit the crime. The punishment corresponded to the value of the goods stolen, and to the amount of damage done in the trespass: the more "valuable" the rape victim, and the more damage done to her property value, the harsher the penalty. And "value", where a woman was concerned, depended strictly upon her economic status as determined by her father or husband, and her desirability as an object of an exclusive sexual relationship.

Thus, the economic position of the rape victim, and her status as a desirable, marriageable property, were the two features assessed in determining the extent of punishment to be meted out to the rape offender. Under Anglo-Saxon law, the higher the economic or social position of the woman's husband or father, the higher the fee exacted from the rapist. And that rule of thumb continued well past the point at which Anglo-Saxon law was superseded by a more sophisticated legal system which moved beyond simple reparation and compensation for offences. The punishment of rape has never lost its connections with the economic status of the rape victim. The higher the socio-economic status of the victim, the greater the likelihood that she will be considered "credible", and granted her day in court. As we have already seen from the data presented, this is as true today as it was six hundred years ago. All that has changed is that the economic position of the victim's husband or father is no longer seen to be the sole measure of her economic worth. With women's greater participation in the productive labour force, some women have begun to earn an economic rating for themselves, and this rating is, as we have seen, reflected in the data presented.

But the relationship between a rape victim and her husband or father is, as we have also seen, by no means irrelevant to the question of whether or not she will be seen as a credible rape victim: those women who are most clearly dependent upon a male owner/protector will most readily be viewed as meriting protection from rape. And the reason for this lies in the popular belief that one of the major attributes of "real" rape is the subsequent diminution of the victim's value as a desirable marriage "partner". From the earliest times to the present, virgins have been considered "credible" rape victims, because the loss of virginity most drastically and obviously affects the social value women have as desirable objects of exclusive sexual access. When a woman's value consists in her sexual and reproductive capacities, and when the object of marriage is to gain access to the *exclusive* use of a woman's sexuality, virginity is, of course, a woman's greatest treasure. Loss of virginity (or, if married, loss of one's status as an object of guaranteed, exclusive sexual access) markedly affects a woman's property value. This is why the law has always favoured rape victims who are virgins under the ownership and protection of their fathers, or chaste wives under the ownership and protection of their husbands. The right of men to preserve valu-able sexual property—either for their own use, or for the use of a husband, in which case the daughter's virginity was a great asset at the bargaining table—was one of the rights which rape laws were meant to protect. It is hardly surprising, therefore, that virgins and chaste wives are the most highly protected forms of sexual property within the system, and that these are the women which the law perceives as credible rape victims. In their endorsement of the idea that virginity and marital chastity are the primary features which give woman value— features which belong to women's husbands or fathers—contemporary rape laws reflect their historical origins.

Rape laws were simply one of the devices designed to secure to men the ownership and control of those forms of property, and to provide a conceptual framework which would justify punishing men who violated the property rights of other men in this respect.

The development of our modern criminal offence of rape began in the Middle Ages as a specific response to the problem of bride capture. Under this system, marriages were frequently accomplished by means of abduction and rape.[8] Sexual intercourse with a woman had long been regarded as establishing a primary right to possession and, ultimately, to ownership through marriage with the woman in question. The legal articulation of an offence of rape was not meant to undermine the validity of this method of establishing a basis for marriage. Abduction and rape remained valid ways of establishing a legal and sanctified marital relationship; indeed, this practice is still followed in many communities, where marriage is often regarded as the only "honourable" course to be followed once a rape has occurred. But rape laws *were* designed to prevent legitimate transfers of property through marriages established this way.

Under the marriage laws of the time, any property which a woman owned , or to which she might become entitled upon marriage (such as a dowry), automatically became the property of her husband. Her rights to such property were, as they say in the legal trade, "extinguished" upon marriage, and for the most part they remained extinguished forever after, although in some few instances they "revived" on the death of her husband.[9] Understandably, fathers had a vested interest in preventing marriages between their daughters and men who had nothing to offer. Men of property with eligible daughters wanted to marry them off in the ways best calculated to secure and, if possible, increase their property holdings. They wanted their daughters to "marry well", and marriages were, at least among the propertied classes, business mergers rather than the wedding of kindred spirits.[10]

In order to prevent unscrupulous and upwardly-mobile men from acquiring rights to family property through abduction and rape, men of property developed rape laws. Rape did not nullify a marriage, but it did nullify the rights of the husband to his wife's property if the marriage was established by this means. Marriage and rape laws were twin mechanisms, designed to ensure that transfers of property would and could be accomplished only in accordance with the express wishes of a woman's father, or of whatever other male had authority over her. The primary function of rape laws, therefore, was to deny rights of ownership in property to men who were not acceptable to the families of the women in question, and who attempted to get around such familial disapproval by abduction and raping the daughter of the family. The secondary function of rape laws was to protect men in their ownership of daughters who were, because of their virginity, valuable properties in their own right. Thus, the social function of rape laws was the protection and preservation of patrimonial property, both in the form of real property (land), and in the form of desirable female sexual property (virgin daughters).

Once rape laws had become effective in preventing unscrupulous men from gaining access to power and position by abducting and raping wealthy heiresses, their chief purpose became the protection of men in their ownership of desirable female sexual property. The only women rape laws were designed to protect were women of high socio-economic status and those who were highly desirable as objects of an exclusive sexual relationship. But since the offence was conceived as a wrong to the man entitled to rights of ownership over a woman, the law did not view her as the party injured by rape. She was, again as they say in the trade, merely a third-party "beneficiary" of the law. She was protected because the law sought to protect men in the ownership of such valuable women, and not because she herself had any right to autonomy—sexual or otherwise—which the law sought to protect. Rape was not perceived as a violation of the rights of women at all, and the present treatment of rape continues to reflect its historical roots. This is precisely why it is that *dependent* women, women living at home under the control of parents, or with a husband, are the rape victims the system most strongly supports. Independent women, on the other hand, are seen as quite literally having no right to complain of rape: since they cannot own themselves, and since rape is an offence against the owner of sexual property, such women are not viewed as having a legitimate complaint if they are raped. Instead, they are viewed as "vindictive" or "unreasonable", unless, of course, they sustained serious and preferably permanent physical damage.

If physical injury does occur, then the law is prepared to take these women seriously because the act can be seen as causing a net loss in their sexual attractiveness, and therefore in their value. In the absence of such disfigurement, however, rape victims who are independent of parental or matrimonial control are not thought to have anything to complain about. They have not suffered a significant loss in their potential to be desirable objects of exclusive sexual access, and no rights of ownership have been infringed. No ownership, no wrong.

In the application of rape laws as infringements of rights of ownership, the legal structure has simply extended the same rules of lawful appropriation to sexual as to other forms of private property. The only property which deserves the full protection of the law is that which is already owned, and the most severe punishments are reserved for offenders who infringe rights of ownership already established by someone else. If presently unowned property is at least potentially valuable, it deserves to be protected from wanton mutilation or destruction. But if an object has no perceivable value, either actual or potential, then no property rights can be violated, and no harm can be done. Only an object with an actual or potential value qualifies for the protection of the law. It makes little difference whether the object in question is a tree in the forest or a woman in the street.

Rape is treated as an offence against the person, as a direct harm to the woman attacked, only if it results in severe injury to the victim, and even then, an evaluation of the victim's "value" affects judgments made about the gravity of the offence. One is regarded as having suffered a harm only if one has lost possession of something valuable, and since a woman's value lies in her desirability as an object of an exclusive sexual relationship, she is not viewed as having suffered a harm if she has already lost that which gave her such a status. This is why a non-virgin is immediately suspect as a credible rape victim, even when she is injured by the attack; and physical injuries are themselves perceived as legitimating her complaint only if they lead to a demonstrable loss in her property value. The degree of physical harm suffered by the victim, and her prior and present value as sexual property, are among the major factors which determine her standing as a credible rape victim. But if she had little sexual value to begin with, and was not seriously injured by the attack, where is the harm in the rape?

the commoditization of female sexuality

However, there is more to the issue of sexual value than has so far been discussed. While it is obvious that loss of virginity is a major setback to women, given that it forever prevents them from being desirable as objects of an *exclusive* sexual relationship, this does not in

itself explain why the law apparently refuses to protect women who
are somewhat more "liberal" in the distribution of their sexuality.
Why is it that certain types of rape victims are popularly viewed as
women who "got what they deserved", "were asking for it", or,
simply, as women who are not credible because of their "prom-
isicuity" or "lewd and unchaste" behaviour? The simple explanation
is that women who voluntarily give up that which makes them
desirable as objects of an exclusive sexual relationship are seen as
"common property", to be appropriated without penalty for the use,
however temporary, of any man who desires their services. What
this public attitude seems to entail is that the voluntary granting of
sexual access outside the parameters of sanctified matrimony leads to
the loss of sexual and physical autonomy. Once a woman parts with
her one and only treasure, she never has the right to say no again.

But that would seem to imply that women have the right to
sexual autonomy at least at some point in their lives. Up to the point
at which virginity is irretrievably lost, a woman may say "yes" or
"no" with some hope that her wishes will be honoured. It is, we
believe, false to construe this as in any way constituting a woman's
right to sexual autonomy. With the conversion of women into forms
of private property, with a value determined by their sexuality,
female sexuality ceased to be a quality over which women exercised
rights of ownership. It became a quality held in trust by their fathers
for their potential husbands, and thus, a quality of themselves which
women also held in trust for their potential owner/husbands. From
that time up to the present, women did not have rights of ownership over their own sexuality and reproductivity. The sexuality of
women became a commodity to be traded on the marriage market,
bargained and paid for in the marriage contract between father and
prospective husband. This is the explanation for the legal qualification
that a husband cannot rape his own wife. What a husband gets when he
gets a wife is rights of ownership in her sexuality, and what this means
is the right to use her sexuality whenever and however he pleases. Her
wishes in the matter are simply irrelevant. Husbands have a legally
protected right to the sexual services of their wives, and wives have a
legal duty to honour the "conjugal rights" of their husbands. Women
certainly do not have sexual autonomy within marriage, and any
question of their "consent" to sexual relations is utterly without
meaning in this context.

Prior to marriage, a woman's sexuality is a commodity to be held in trust for its lawful owner. Making a "free" use of one's sexuality is like making a "free" use of someone else's money. One can act autonomously only with things that belong to oneself. Things held in trust for others are surrounded with special duties which place the trustee under strict obligations for the care and maintenance of the assets in question, and also place the trustee under a strict duty to avoid unreasonable risks. If I hold money in trust for someone else, any act of mine which diminishes the assets held, other than those expenses necessarily incurred for its preservation and increase, is an act of theft. I am legally prohibited from using the assets to further my own interest, and must justify all actions involving the assets as being in the interest of the person for whom the trust is established. And so it is with female sexuality. Women are not regarded as being entitled to use their sexuality according to their own desires because their sexuality is not theirs to use for such purposes. Their duty is to preserve it in the best possible condition for the ultimate use and disposition of its rightful owner. Thus, women who behave in a sexually autonomous manner are stealing from those to whom their sexuality properly belongs, and are no more deserving of protection or redress than persons who are free spenders with other people's money. They are to be punished rather than protected.

Moreover, just as trustees are legally prohibited from taking unreasonable risks with the assets they hold, so women are expected to avoid taking any risks with their sexuality. Women who place themselves in "compromising" situations, who frequent "low" areas of the city or associate with "undesirables", are seen as taking risks with themselves which they ought not to take, and as being either reckless or negligent in the protection of that which they have a duty to preserve. Since the taking of unreasonable risks means that the victim contributes to the commission of the offence by assumption of the risk, she is regarded as being undeserving of redress in the event that the risk materializes. This is what lies behind the popular phrase: "she got what she deserved". Women who place their sexuality in jeopardy do not deserve protection because they are doing something which they ought not do in the first place; and if they are raped they deserve no redress, because they voluntarily incurred the risk. So the theory goes. Women who use their sexuality as they themselves desire, who appropriate to themselves an alleged right to sexual autonomy, are "outlaws" and "renegades". They are making free with a commodity which they have no right to dispense, and therefore they fall well beyond the definition of the "respectable" women who were meant to be the beneficiaries of rape laws. For in the end, "respectable" women are just women who agree to live by the rules of the society in which they find themselves, who regard themselves as wives and mothers, who accept their status as forms of private property and relinquish any claim to ownership rights in their own sexuality and reproductive ability. Women who refuse to accept these rules and limitations are viewed as relinquishing any right to be protected, and are thereby punished for making that choice.

the open territory victim

Refusing to abide by the rules is tantamount to accepting for oneself a status as "valueless", and entails that one can fairly be regarded as "common property", up for grabs by any man who wants sexual contact. As the data clearly shows, the law gives little protection to women who are judged to be "valueless", and what leads to that judgment is having broken free of parental or matrimonial control, and of having tried to be autonomous, sexually and otherwise. The law does not penalize men for appropriating what is regarded as abandoned or "common" sexual property any more than it penalizes them for appropriating other forms of abandoned or unowned property. So it is that "promiscuous" women, women who are "idle", "unemployed" or "on welfare", living "common law", "separated" or "divorced", "known frequenters of Yorkville", "drug users", "alcoholics", or "incorrigible", are all perceived as women who are *not* credible rape victims, for they have all, by their behaviour, placed themselves at risk and hence forfeited any right to either protection or redress. And these "valueless" women are real persons; they are the women we described in chapter 5 as the "women who can't be raped", women whose cases are classified as unfounded because the police know that they will not make "convincing" witnesses in court.

It is virtually impossible for these women to complain of rape and have their complaint taken seriously. Because they are perceived to be valueless, a rapist may attack them with impunity, without fear of either retribution or rebuke. They are perceived as women who take unreasonable risks, who ought to know what they are getting into, who may drink in bars and even go home with the men they meet there, who solicit or accept rides from strangers. And if the worst happens, then the risk which was taken must have been unreasonable. And so, the victim is construed as being responsible for her own disaster. Open territory victims, then, are women with an already diminished sexual and reproductive value, or women who have forfeited this value by defying traditional expectations of respectable, acceptable, female behaviour. This flaunting of tradition is no mere social impropriety, but a direct threat to the stability of the sexual *status quo*. As the champion of all forms of the *status quo,* the law cannot protect these women against rape. It will either ignore their complaints, on the rationale that nothing of value has been lost, or penalize them even further for placing themselves at risk and wilfully damaging that which gave them a property value.

But as is clear from this discussion, the present treatment and handling of rape and rape victims within the Canadian criminal justice system does not arise from any malfunction in the administration of the law or any gross bias on the part of those who administer the system. Given the conceptual framework out of which rape laws developed, and within which rape evolved as a criminal offence, the results are exactly what we would expect. Rape laws were never meant to protect all women from rape, or to provide women with any guaranteed right to sexual autonomy. Rape laws were designed to preserve valuable female sexual property for the exclusive ownership of those men who could afford to acquire and maintain it. Thus, it is not at all surprising that the present practices are what they are given the historical context of the legal offence of rape.

The system of inequalities which has determined the formulation and application of rape laws is also, we believe, the root cause of rape itself. Women and men do not face each other as equals in our society, and their sexual relations are scarcely ever a simple expression of mutual sexual interest in one another. Sexual relationships are inextricably bound up with economic relationships of dependency and ownership, and very often they involve some kind of trade-off, calculation or coercion. As we shall discuss in the next chapter, rape is only an extreme manifestation of the coercive sexuality that pervades our entire culture. It is an inescapable by-product of a system in which sexual relationships are also power relationships, in which female sexuality is a commodity, and in which some men have no source of power except physical force. The logical conclusion of this analysis is that in order to eliminate rape, we must alter the underlying social structure which produces it.

8
coercive sexuality and female sexual property

In the last chapter we provided a theoretical analysis of the historical position of women. What we wish to consider in this chapter is the impact that this position still has on the day-to-day experience of women. Women's status as forms of private property, with their primary value deriving from their sexual and reproductive functions, is not just a useful theoretical construct which helps us to understand what we are; it is also a fact and a present reality which exercises a continuing and pervasive influence on our lives. The consequences of this fact are immense. The central core of both male and female socialization is internalization of the belief that women's sexual and reproductive functions are not their own property, and that rights over the distribution of female sexuality and reproduction lie in the hands of women's male owners.

Women learn first that their sexuality is under the control of their fathers, who are duty-bound to ensure that it is kept intact for their daughters' future husbands. Female sexuality belongs to an actual or potential husband, and those entrusted with the control of a woman prior to her marriage have an obligation to ensure her virginal status. Insofar as possible, socialization processes attempt to internalize this value in the female, to make her accept the "fact" that her sexuality is something which she holds in trust for someone else, her potential husband. Reliance on external threats of parental, particularly paternal, wrath is a secondary back-up which comes into play if the internalized standards flag. Most women do accept, at least to some degree, the concept that their sexuality is something which is not theirs, but which they hold in trust. Fortunately, many never progress beyond understanding that it is something which others, paricularly their fathers, *think* they should hold in trust, but even this inhibition is enough to ensure that women do not dispose of their sexuality purely in accordance with their own desires. Most women do not exercise either their sexual or their reproductive capacities freely for the simple reason that you cannot give freely what you do not believe rightfully belongs to you.

Because their sexuality is not theirs to use at their pleasure, but something to be owned by and held in trust for others, women are forced to be sexually manipulative in order to secure their own interests. They are also socialized to regard this as appropriately "feminine" behaviour. Control through the offer, hint, or suggestion of sexual favours, or through the denial of sexual contact are the dominant modes women are expected and socialized to adopt in pursuit of their goals. But inherent in this process are certain risks. One learns at an early age to be careful in the use of sexually manipulative techniques, and as with all techniques, one becomes more skillful in their deployment with increasing experience. This places the "beginners", young women, in a particularly vulnerable position; they are just learning to use the techniques available to them, but must do so without adequate knowledge of the risks to which particular strategies leave them open.

Thus, conventional relations between the sexes force women to take certain risks with their sexuality while at the same time exercising special care to preserve their inviolate virginity and "good" reputation. As in any risk situation, some bad risks must inevitably be realized. But from the perspective of men, who expect women to act as the trustees of their own sexuality, almost any risk is an unreasonable risk—and risk is frequently judged with the wisdom of hindsight. If you were raped, then you must have taken a risk, and since you are duty-bound not to take risks, then it is your own fault if you were raped. This is the prevailing logic, despite the fact that women have no choice but to take such risks if they are to "capitalize" on the only assets they are seen to have at their disposal.

If all women were to refuse to take the kinds of risks which filter rape cases out of the criminal justice system, however, many of the more usual forms of social contact between the sexes would be eliminated. It is *unreasonable* to expect women to avoid *reasonable* risks. While it may in some sense be irrational for women to take unreasonable risks, not even the taking of an unreasonable risk should subject them to physical attack without rights of redress; it would not do so except for the belief that women are responsible for their own protection and are therefore to be censured if they engage in risk-taking which has bad results. Rape is virtually a strict liability offence. Were it not for the expectation that women should exercise an exceptionally high standard of care over their sexuality, we would not expect them never to place themselves in an even potentially "dangerous" situation. And we would not have such expectations if we believed that women's sexuality was rightfully theirs, to own and control.

Nor would women need to be sexually manipulative if their sexuality were not regarded as their basic stock-in-trade. But it is an indisputable fact that women *do* become socialized to accept the view that they cannot make free use of their sexuality or their reproductive ability. Women almost always feel guilty about having sexual relations with anyone other than their actual husbands, the men to whom they are engaged, or, at least, the men with whom they are "in love" or having a "serious" relationship. And the only explanation for this guilt is their acceptance, however unconscious, of the belief that their sexuality is something they hold in trust for the mythical Mr. Right. And so it is with reproduction. In our culture, one of the prime signs of "real love" is the desire to have Mr. Right's babies; correspondingly, Mr. Right knows that he has found his woman when he wants her to have his children. (A woman almost never has *her* children, but almost always has *his* children.) These features of our experience all indicate the deep conditioning which has gone into having us accept our status as sexual and reproductive property.

And because women only have their sexual and reproductive capacities to offer on the market, since these are the only qualities which give them property value, they must indeed bargain with them. Women must make the best bargain possible, using their present assets as surety against future financial, emotional, and sexual insecurity. The man tries to get the best bargain possible, and the woman tries to spend as little of her stock-in-trade as she can; she doles out her trust in the hope that it will be going to its rightful owner, or that the loss will be so minimal that the future owner either won't notice or won't mind. But sexually speaking, because men and women do not bargain from positions of equality, all of the sexual transactions between them are potentially coercive in nature, and many of them are in fact so. The act of rape is simply a product of such sexual coercion.

Given that women are placed in the contradictory position of having to use the reward of sexual contact or the threat of sexual deprivation in order to get what they want, and of being regarded as under a special obligation to devote themselves to the minimization of threats to their sexual purity, it is no surprise to find that men have to persuade and coerce women into parting with their sexual favours. In return for the favours granted, men must offer women at least some promise of protection, and since women believe that their sexuality rightfully belongs only to their actual or potential husband, men must present themselves to women as actual or potential husbands. The problems for women are bad enough even when men sincerely present themselves as potential husbands, but they are immense when the man involved has absolutely no intention of being anybody's husband, at this particular point in his life.

From the male point of view, female sexuality is a commodity in the possession of women, even if it is something men will come to own and control under the appropriate circumstances. Women are seen as the hoarders and miserly dispensers of a much desired commodity, and men must constantly wheedle, bargain, and pay a price for what they want. And if anything lies at the root of misogyny, this does. Men naturally come to resent and dislike women because they see them as having something which they want and have a perfect right to, but which women are unwilling to give them freely. The right to female sexuality must be purchased.

Woman's alienation from her own sexuality, man's resentment at having to purchase sexual fulfillment, the unequal bargaining that trades security for sex—all of these distortions of human sexuality make it inevitable that much sexual contact between men and women will necessarily be coercive in nature. Women must withold sex from men, and men must pay women a price for it. The top price is marriage, but women may also exchange their sexuality for emotional security, social status, minor economic rewards, or, more negatively, safety from economic or physical threats. If men are unable or unwilling to pay the top price, they must bargain women down. If they still do not have the assets to purchase the sexual property they want, they must persuade or force women into parting with it. Of course, even the "best" bargain a woman can make is fundamentally coercive, since it entails an acceptance of herself as property, and is made from a position of inequality.

The coercive methods which men use may range from mild persuasion to blatant physical force. A man may pretend he is willing to pay the highest price for a woman's sexuality, by offering marriage, or "stringing her a line". He may use economic inducements: a raise, presents, an "expensive date". Or, he may use obviously coercive tactics: general harassment, the old "come across or walk" routine, threats of physical harm or death.

The tactics of coercion which a man uses will depend on the personal assets which he has at hand. If he is good-looking, rich and powerful, he may "charm" a woman into sleeping with him. If he is less attractive or successful, he may have to rely on intimidation to achieve the sexual contact he desires. Men must develop strategies for getting what they want, preferably without paying the highest market price, and these strategies will vary according to the commodity's price, their evaluation of the individual woman's worth, and their own socio-economic status and conditioning.

Many men lack the purchasing power to buy the sexual property they want, at least at some point in their lives, and some men will take what they want, if they cannot get it freely and cannot (or will not) pay the price demanded. If they do not have the money, power or prestige necessary to win a woman's consent, then men will use physical force to take the sexuality they desire. It is not surprising, therefore, that most of what is labelled "rape" is committed by working-class men who do not have the ability to use middle-class strategies of persuasion and economic inducement. Middle-class men desire the same object as working-class men, but they need not resort to "illegitimate" means to procure it. Physical force is simply the method used by men who lack other, subtler means of sexual coercion.

Nor is it surprising that rapists from low socio-economic backgrounds should frequently choose middle-class women as their victims. In a society which allots women different price-tags, it is inevitable that some women will be too expensive for some men, but that those men will nonetheless desire what they cannot afford. Some of these men will take what they want; they literally *steal* the female sexuality they desire because they lack the necessary social and economic means of acquiring it legitimately.

rape: *the limit on acceptable sexual coercion*

The behavior prohibited by the laws against rape is merely the least acceptable form of sexual trading, and in our allegedly highly advanced and civilized stage of development, it is the one form of such trading which we bar as illegal. Other forms of trading, no matter how frankly fraudulent or exploitive are tolerated as part of our way of life; only forcible intercourse is socially and legally unacceptable. Beyond that, it is a free market, and like most supposedly free markets, it operates to the disadvantage of those who are least favoured to begin with, who do not begin from a position of equality in the bargaining relationship.

What we call "rape" is only that form of sexual coercion which is accompanied by the use or threat of physical force. In treating rape as a grave moral offence, and in punishing those whom we find guilty of it, we do not punish sexual coercion as such but only one particular form of it. We do not punish the end, the achievement of sexual contact through coercion, but only the means used to achieve that end. And we do this without even considering whether physical coercion is the most *harmful* form of such coercion. This is like attaching grave moral harm to murder, and severely punishing those whom we find guilty of it, while letting drunk and reckless drivers kill thousands of people on the highways with no such retributive consequences or moral disapprobation. Since we have accepted the motor car as an indispensable part of life, we are prepared to tolerate all but the most reckless forms of behaviour that go with it, and since we have accepted coercive sexuality as an inevitable way of life, we are prepared to accept all but its most physically abusive expressions.

Within the technical limits of the term, rape will always be an inevitable consequence of the fact that some men do not have the means to achieve sexual relations with women, except through physical violence. From the perspective of women, of course, there is much more rape than that which is technically classified as "rape" because many of the sexual acts which are forced upon them pose grave threats, and at the very least minimize their opportunity to be self-determining, independent human beings. But even much of what would be legally classifiable as "rape" goes unreported and unpunished because of male preconceptions about what constitutes "legitimate" seduction. It is only when physical harm or threats of physical harm are inflicted that society is prepared to step in to reprimand the offender. As they now stand, rape laws articulate only the rock-bottom standards of sexually coercive behaviour.

Because women are forms of private property, with a property value determined by their sexual and reproductive capacities, much of the sexual contact between men and women is necessarily and fundamentally coercive. The persuasive/coercive tactics used by men will be inevitable as long as women do not have the right to sexual and reproductive autonomy—both legally, and in terms of the actual consequences free disposition of their sexual and reproductive capacities would entail. Sexual coercion, its reality and necessity, are thus deeply rooted in our history, in our basic social, political, economic, and legal system. And rape is one of the prices which we must pay for that system.

9
rapists
and other normal men

In reading past literature on rape and the rape offender, one quickly realizes the extent to which research conclusions have been shaped by the concepts and attitudes which investigators brought with them to their work. Academic research into rape has been predicated on the common belief that there are really two kinds of rape: "real rape" and "everyday rape". "Real rape" is a gross violation of our most elementary moral principles, and the serious crime that our laws against rape were meant to prohibit. In its purest form it is virgin-rape, the brutal defloration of an innocent maiden. This stereotype owes much to the legacy of rape as a property offence, which defines rape as an attack on a respectable woman by a man with no legal claim to her sexuality.

Needless to say, "real rape" is comparatively rare, though it is the standard against which all alleged rapes are measured. Most of the rapes encountered in the criminal justice system do not fit the myth which has been handed down to us: they may involve "promiscuous" women and fairly average men; their circumstances may be perceived as inflammatory, or leading "naturally" to the event. This type of "everyday rape" is not regarded as a serious criminal offence, but as an understandable result of the usual forms of contact between the sexes. At most, it is seen as a mildly delinquent act. And like the public at large, social scientists have viewed rape in an ambivalent manner, judging only some acts of forcible sexual intercourse to be "real rape". Similarly, they have brought the general stereotype of the "real rapist" to their research.

the rape offender and mental abnormality

In the public imagination, the rapist is pictured as a misshapen satyr with pointed ears and cloven hoofs. He is consumed with lust, and totally unable to control his animal passions. The rapist represents the negative side of the masculine principle, in which lust is untempered by reason, and desire unmediated by morality. The crime which he commits is the worst crime of all, for it destroys the positive side of the feminine principle, in which lust is non-existent and desire is strictly controlled. The rapist is the embodiment of human evil, his victim is the embodiment of moral perfection, and his crime is the archetype of primal violence.

This view of the rapist as a true moral monster also lay behind the early studies of rape. Modern psychiatry attempted to transform the rapist into a victim of mental illness (thereby removing the stigma of free choice from his behaviour), but accepted his basic image unchallenged. While the rapist was now regarded as sick, rather than evil, his features remained the same.

In the first blush of therapeutic approaches to crime, the rapist was subjected to the standard battery of psychiatric tests and examinations. He was expected to be grossly abnormal, suffering from a deep-seated psychiatric disorder which could explain his actions. On the whole, however, the results of these tests were negative.[1] It is true that some of the earliest studies suggested abnormality in the rapist, but most of these studies dealt with the general category of "sexual offenders" and did not distinguish rapists from exhibitionists, paedophiles, or voyeurs.[2] When the results of studies differentiating the rapist from other sexual offenders began to come in, the rapist was found to be relatively normal, according to the standards used by the researchers. Some researchers found rapists to display "inadequate personalities" or "sociopathic tendencies",[3] but none discovered that gross abnormality which had been anticipated.[4]

The concept of "normality" used by social scientists is itself something of a puzzle, however. Virtually all studies have found the rapist to manifest great hostility towards women, but no one has been prepared to classify misogyny as mental *illness*. The general conclusion has been that the vast majority of rapists do not have a "treatable mental illness", and are suffering from nothing more severe than a "character disorder".

Despite these findings, the stereotypical image of the rapist has never seriously been questioned in the social sciences. When researchers found that their assumptions about rapists were not confirmed by the data, they did not reject the myth of the "real rapist". Instead, they re-assessed the reality and importance of most reported rapes. The stereotype of the "real rapist" has been left intact, and no attempt has been made to develop a theory of rape which could explain the behaviour of rapists.

Nevertheless, the discovery that the rapist is "normal" has had a significant impact on general attitudes towards rape, both in the academic community and in the courts. Its main effect has been to undermine even further the status of rape as a serious offence. If most rape offenders do not fit the picture of the "real rapist", then it follows that their crime is not "real rape" but only a misdemeanor of the everyday variety. Of course, most reported rapes had never measured up to the myth of "real rape", but a gloss of scientific legitimacy was now added to their dismissal as trivial events.

This realignment of attitudes towards rape and the rapist has had at least one practical consequence for rape offenders and their victims. Because the rapist does not display extreme abnormality, he has not been judged a danger to the community, and he has not, therefore, been subjected to the kind of controls reserved for those who are seen in this way. "Real rape" may itself still be seen as a serious moral crime, but when the rapist exhibits nothing more disturbing than hostility towards women, he is not regarded as seriously ill, or subjected to the restriction of liberty which we reserve for those who are so afflicted.[5] From the point of view of victims, it means that unless their attackers are diagnosably mentally ill, there is little chance that the injury will be redressed.

It appears that our society is prepared to tolerate rape as long as it is not committed by the certifiably mentally ill. If those who commit rape are not mentally ill, then we have no right to intervene very noticeably in their lives. The mental illness of the rapist, rather than the fact that he has committed rape, is taken as the relevant signal that he may be a threat to society. We can only wonder at the theoretical assumptions which would justify taking motivation rather than behaviour as a reasonable indicator of future risk, and are almost driven to lament the fact that the studies did not consistently reveal the rapist to be a raving psychotic.

In fact, the research has shown the rapist to be remarkably similar to the average heterosexual male. Some studies have shown rapists to be significantly different from other sexual offenders, such as paedophiles,[6] but only in the sense that they can be used as a reliable control group to isolate particular variables. In other words, a group of rapists would be just as effective a control group for isolating variables characteristic of the paedophile as any other group of non-paedophiliac males, including "normal" males. The results of these studies seem to be consistent with the findings of Pascal and Herzberg, that there is a total lack of differentiation between rapists and a control group over a wide range of variables; indeed, "the controls and rapists are indistinguishable from one another". Pascal and Herzberg conclude that "if we take heterosexual behaviour between adults as our standard, then it is difficult to see how rapists differ from the controls in sexual behaviour *per se*."[7]

misogyny and the "normal" male

What the social scientists have given us, then, is the insight that the rapist is no different from other heterosexual males whose chosen sexual objects are adult women. But they have also given us a rather revealing picture of what they accept as a "normal" heterosexual male. If a marked hostility towards women is not enough to denote mental illness—to distinguish an abnormal male personality from a normal one—then obviously a certain degree of hostility towards women is considered to be well within normal limits. Since none of the investigators were prepared to say that even extreme misogyny is abnormal, then all must agree that some degree of misogyny is quite normal.

However, if anyone had suggested to these researchers that misandry is a normal characteristic of the adult female, they would have concluded that the speaker was a lunatic. The label "man-hater" has always been an insult to women, and more recently, misandry has been taken as a manifestation of mental illness, of that unresolved penis-envy which can cause women to disavow their "natural" role. To be a man-hater is to be an unnatural female, in need of psychiatric help, but to be a woman-hater is to be a natural, normal male.

Not only is it regarded as normal for men to be misogynists, it is also regarded as normal for women to be misogynists. Many women admit that they do not like other women very much, and their preference for male company is not regarded as unnatural. But, of course, the converse is not true. It is unusual for men to like women, except as sex objects, and it would not be considered either healthy or normal for a man to prefer the company of women.

The root of misogyny, as we have discussed in the previous chapter, lies in men's resentment at having to bargain with women for sexual gratification. It is hardly surprising, therefore, that this misogyny should be most dramatically expressed by men without the economic or social means to acquire the women they want. But while the necessity for such bargaining is the root cause of male misogyny, it is not the only factor which contributes to it. However justified men may believe their social position to be, they are nonetheless aware, at some level, that women are oppressed and do not always accept their oppression willingly. Misogyny is caused by fear as well as resentment, and as the Orpheus legend tells us, many men fear women deeply. There is always a possibility that the submissive housewife may turn into a bacchante or Medea, or (according to a more modern legend), a "castrating female".

No analogous myth or psychological concept expresses women's fear of men, because our cultural symbols have been created by men and express the male point of view. Even that quasi-historical legend, "the rape of the Sabine women", tells us how men, and not women, felt about this particular method of founding a new political order. (One can only conjecture that the women involved did not think too highly of the order thus established!) The acceptance of misogyny as normal is just one example of the way in which ideological concepts provide the underpinnings of existing power relations. The belief in "normal misogyny" makes misogyny both acceptable and invisible, rendering its worst effects less serious in the public view. In this way, rape becomes a "non-problem".

Another ideological belief that supports sexual inequality is the myth of the "protective male". Women are not supposed to fear men, but to regard them as their protectors against the dangers of this world—including rape. This dictum is difficult to square with the historical facts. As McCaldon remarks,

> Rape, as part of the natural booty of conquest, has been tolerated from antiquity up to recent times....[8]

(Tolerated by whom, one might well ask!) McCaldon goes on to claim that "today the armed forces of civilized nations do not rape captive women".[9] Tell that to the women of Bangladesh and Viet Nam —though one might argue about which nations are civilized and which are not. But rape is a continuing historical reality for women, and not just a consequence of war. Women are raped every day, by strangers, acquaintances, friends, uncles and fathers. While the whole weight of social conditioning reinforces the stereotype of men as strong and protective, and of women as weak and vulnerable, women are also taught, and learn very quickly, to be afraid of men. Any woman who is at all able to learn by means of the empirical method, soon learns to fear men. The concept of man–as–protector has its threatening dimension, for it acknowledges that men are also the danger from which women need protection. We are taught that men will protect us, but that in order to qualify for such protection, we must do as we are told; the penalty for refusing to accept our appointed role is physical and social abuse.

Thus, women are simultaneously socialized to trust men and to rely on them, and not to trust them and not to take the risk of relying on them. Depending on a particular woman's background, one side of this ambivalent message will prevail, and a source of severe emotional trauma to some rape victims is their deep sense of betrayal. These are the women who have been successfully conditioned to trust men. To be catapulted from a naive belief in the protective role of men into a full-blown realization that some men are predators and anything but trustworthy, is a very hard reality for some women to accept because it calls into question their basic identity as women. What woman wants to continue seeing herself as weak and vulnerable, when she has learned that she can no longer expect men to protect her? It takes time to rebuild a self-image, and it is not surprising that some rape victims take months or even years to "get over" the rape. What they are "getting over" is not just the rape, but the awful awareness that they were taken in by a role identity which left them defenceless against those whom they had been taught to trust.

At the general level, women's socialization to seek male protectors is simply a "protection racket" on a grand scale, for the price of protection (from men themselves) is appropriation. Women must be socialized to trust men, for their ultimate destiny is to be owned and protected by one of them. But women must also be socialized to fear men, lest they lose that sexual virtue which alone gives them property value.

The stereotypes of men as strong and dominant, and of women as weak and vulnerable, make the protection of women by men seem legitimate and "natural". But there is an unexplained gap between protection and property. Even if women do need protection, it does not follow that they must be converted into forms of private property in order to be protected, or indeed, that their conversion into private property really affords them the best possible protection. And if men didn't use their greater physical strength to brutalize women, women would not need protection in the first place. But the conventional stereotypes of male and female nature, like the "normality" of misogyny and the "abnormality" of misandry, are merely used to justify and perpetuate the domination of women by men in our society.

Men's fear of women, and the misogyny it produces, rests on the awareness that women have good reason to seek revenge, and on the pure abstract possibility that women would revenge themselves on men if they could. But if our society were not controlled by men, and if men did not rape women and otherwise brutalize them, men would have no need to fear those whom they now oppress. Equality leaves no basis for either fear or resentment, and the belief that misogyny is normal reflects nothing other than a belief in sexual inequality. In our culture, a "normal male" equals a "male who is superior to females". As long as that belief exists, misogyny is inevitable, but misogyny can be regarded as "normal" only insofar as we believe that men truly are superior to women.

Women, on the other hand, are treated as irrational if they are misandrists, despite the solid empirical basis for their fear of men. But to allow that this fear is justified would be to give the lie to "natural" sexual inequality. Women are supposed to accept their inferior status because they genuinely are inferior, and not simply because they are

compelled to do so. To regard misandry as normal, would be to acknowledge that misandry is justified. Since it is, in fact, true that our
society discriminates against women, it is also true that women fear
and resent men. But even though it is both rational and culturally
adaptive for women to fear men, misandry is regarded as "abnormal".

The concept of the "normal" male thus contains a built-in
rationale for continuing to oppress women; and normality in the adult
male includes a commitment to misogyny, while normality in the
adult female contains an acceptance of her oppression. Though misogyny, and the sexual aggression which it engenders, are most visible
in the rapist's behaviour, they also characterize the behaviour of
"normal" adult men.

the relativity of seduction

But of course most men are not labelled rapists, and most men do not
believe that they are even potential rapists. Why not? This is surely the
conclusion they should reach. If misogyny and sexual aggression are
the rule rather than the exception, then why are not all men seen as real
or potential rapists? The answer lies, of course, in the legal definition
of rape. "Rape" is only that particular form of sexual coercion which
consists in the use or threat of physical force, and rapists are distinguished from other men only insofar as they use physical coercion to
achieve their desired goal.

Men who use other forms of sexual coercion are not, by definition, rapists, and they would never compare themselves to rapists
because they perceive their actions as *seductions*. These men may use
fraud, economic threats, or the tantalization of economic gain to
coerce their victims, but unless they use physical force their action is
unredressable seduction, no matter how threatened their victims may
be by the coercive methods used to gain their "co-operation". A good
case in point is the story of Martin Evans, a man who "bedded" a
young woman after telling her that he was a psychologist doing
research. The judge held that Evans was not guilty of rape, even
though the victim's consent had been achieved by fraud. He stated that
a man may use any nonviolent means, "even deceit", to get a woman
to say "yes", and, he added, "Bachelors and other men on the make,
fear not. It is not illegal to feed a girl a line." Evans' own comment is
significant: "I seduce; I don't rape".[10]

But even the use of physical force is sometimes seen as legitimate seduction, particularly when the man is better placed in the social hierarchy than the woman. One rape victim in our study was described by the police as "idle", and a frequenter of the old Yorkville area of Toronto; she felt that the man had "gone too far". Another victim sagely remarked that "usually guys stop when you tell them to. This one didn't." In both of these cases, the men were from middle-class backgrounds (one was a businessman, and the other a semi-professional) while the women involved were what we have described as "open territory victims". Neither of these men were charged with rape, because the reporting officers decided not to classify these cases as founded. If the cases had gone to trial, these offenders would not have been perceived as the type of men who would need to use physical violence, and their victims would not have been perceived as the type of women who deserved protection. However, it should be pointed out that in both these cases, the police took the offenders into custody and warned them about what would happen to them if they persisted in this type of behaviour. This merely underlines the extent to which the police are constrained to find informal methods of dealing with offenders they know to be guilty because they also know they would not be found guilty by the formal procedures.

It is hardly surprising that there should be such widespread confusion over the distinction between rape and seduction, given the legitimacy of sexual coercion in our society. The socialization of both men and women takes coercive sexuality as the normal standard of sexual behaviour. Men are expected to apply a certain amount of pressure to have women submit ("agree") to sexual intercourse, and women are expected to resist such pressure, whatever their own desires might happen to be. Men are expected to be sexually dominant and to initiate sexual activity; women are expected to be somewhat passive and to agree to sex with reluctance. Understandably, those men who most strongly identify masculinity with sexual dominance and aggression, are not likely to see any difference between what they call seduction and women call rape.[11]

This situation is not helped by the popular myth that many women have rape fantasies, and even "prefer" rape to non-coercive sex. No woman who has thought seriously about rape can share that belief. Many women have seduction fantasies, but none have rape fantasies—the point of difference being that women do not fantasize being "taken" *against their will,* even if their fantasies involve some degree of physical violence. It is easy for men to transform forcible intercourse into seduction by invoking the myth of women's rape fantasies, but clearly they cannot have it both ways. Either women desire seduction, or women desire rape, but men cannot claim that women "really" desire rape even though "we" men believe it to be merely seduction.

It is this kind of double-think around seduction and rape which allows men to continue seeing their behaviour as seduction no matter what women think about it. Men are not even prepared to abide by the standards which they themselves have established, and classify many acts as seduction even when they fall within the legal definition of rape. Of course, they are even less critical of other forms of sexual coercion.

Men are unwilling to acknowledge that there is anything abnormal about wanting sexual relations with an unwilling partner, because they fear that if full, consensual sexuality were to become the standard of acceptable sexual relations, they would be deprived of many —perhaps most—of the sexual acts which they now enjoy. Men know that in many sexual transactions the woman is not freely consenting but is in some sense "giving in" or being "taken in" by the promise of future reward. Most men would prefer sex with a willing partner, but they realize how rarely women display that full, voluntary desire and participation which should be the ideal. Thus, it is merely a matter of degree. It is normal to desire sexual union with a consenting female, but it is not abnormal to desire sexual union with a female who is not quite consenting. And as we have shown, even the convicted rapist refuses to acknowledge his behaviour as morally wrong. In many cases, he will attempt to characterize it as permissible seduction rather than as prohibited rape.

the relativity of the law

From the victim's point of view, the legal distinction between rape and seduction can be an arbitrary one. To begin with, the law prohibits only one form of sexual coercion—that accomplished through the use or threat of physical force. But secondly, the courts apply even this distinction in an arbitrary and *ad hoc* manner.

Juries have traditionally been composed primarily of middle-class, "respectable" men who share the values underlying rape as an offence against property. Their main concern, in reaching a verdict, is to decide whether this particular defendant used *unacceptable* tactics of sexual coercion on this particular victim. This means, of course, tactics which are unacceptable to them, not to the complainant. Did this man use or threaten physical force to accomplish his objective? The jury's judgment is usually one of probability: is this the kind of man who would use physical force if all else failed? Even coerced intercourse is only classified as rape if it involves physical violence. As a result, the only men who are labelled "rapists" are those men with a limited repertoire, who lack the power, money or training to employ more sophisticated strategies of persuasion/coercion.

This is simply to penalize the man without *savoir faire* or other exploitable resources, while condoning the behaviour of more privileged men. The accused rapist who conforms to the image of "born loser" is most likely to be convicted in court, but the man who presents an appearance of confidence, competence and sophistication is less likely to be perceived as a rapist. If a man has the attributes of success—status, a good job, an attractive wife and family—a jury will find it hard to believe that he would resort to unacceptable tactics of coercion. The labelled rapist is low man on the male totem pole, and he is labelled as much for his status as for his behaviour.

But even the use of physical force is not enough to ensure conviction; the courts also base their judgments on the relative status of the victim and the defendant. Did the accused by his actions, inflict serious damage on a "valuable" woman, or violate the property rights of others? Juries will not condemn the use of physical violence on a categorical basis; their verdicts reflect their judgment of this man and this woman, in this particular situation.

Like most men, jurors are reluctant to acknowledge the existence or the unacceptability of sexual coercion in everyday sexual relations. Those men involved in the judicial process—fathers, husbands, police officers, physicians, lawyers, judges and jurymen—all assume that the defendant before them desires the same object as every other man, and that men "normally" apply pressure to women to achieve sexual contact. The question in their minds, therefore, is whether the evidence overwhelmingly proves that this man used unacceptably coercive tactics to achieve sexual contact with a respectable woman. The issues to be decided are not merely consent or physical force; the jurors' verdict reflects their own self-interest, and their value judgments on the particular individuals involved in the case.

rape and normal motivation

In their reluctance to see everyday rape as "real", the courts have undoubtedly been influenced by the finding that the rapist is not grossly abnormal. It should not be assumed, however, that all rapists fit a single profile or are motivated solely by perfectly normal desires for sexual gratification. Though some feminists have clearly been mistaken in viewing all rapists as "power-trippers", it is true that some rapists are more strongly motivated by the desire to express power over women, than by the simple desire for sexual intercourse. As one convicted rapist volunteered: "You don't want to rape someone just for the orgasm. You want to hurt a woman."[12]

The serious question this raises is, how can such motivation be regarded as normal? The present perspective in the social sciences sees all but the most severely deranged rapists as normal, even though many rapists *prefer* sexual intercourse accompanied by physical violence. Most persons regard the desire for sexual intercourse with animals or dead bodies as an abnormal desire: the desire is abnormal because the object of desire is abnormal. But if the object of normal desire is a willing partner, how can one conclude that the desire for intercourse with a clearly non-consenting female is normal? Why have researchers been unwilling to see offenders of this sort as suffering from mental disorder?

The answer takes us back to two earlier points: the assumed normality of male misogyny, and the coercive sexuality which pervades our entire culture. Most men are misogynists because they see women as the hoarders of an attractive commodity which they desperately desire. In order to achieve sexual gratification, men feel they must necessarily employ coercive tactics of one sort or another. Thus, the man who openly admits wanting to hurt, degrade or humiliate women may be viewed as something of an aberration, but he is not so far out of the ordinary as to be called "abnormal".

The rapist may be unusual insofar as he chooses physical force as his method of sexual coercion, but there is no set of psychological characteristics which sets him clearly apart from other men. All men are shaped by the same social conditioning (though their particular background may modulate their individual response), and they are all sexually coercive to some degree—at least, at some point in their lives. In varying measure, all men accept sexual aggression as part of their masculine identity, though middle and upper-class men may express their power over women through social and economic intimidation. Thus, the rapist is "normal" because he expresses the same *range* of identification with sexual aggression as men in general.

The crucial point to consider, however, is that current definitions of "normality" and "abnormality" have been drawn up within a framework of coercive sexuality which is the accepted standard of behaviour. Until we examine that framework, as well as the variations within it, we cannot begin to understand the real similarities and differences between the labelled rapist and other men.

the reality of "everyday rape"

The finding that the rapist is "normal" served to trivialize the problem of rape in the social sciences, in the courts, and in the public mind. Surprisingly, it did not seem to affect public judgments about the nature and gravity of "real rape"; it merely reinforced the view that most acts which are called "rape" are not really rape. The concept of rape as an explosive manifestation of sexual evil still prevails, and in our view, this perpetuation of the stereotype has been responsible for the reassessment—and dismissal—of most rape cases reported to the police.

The myth of "real rape" is fostered by sensational newspaper accounts of rapes which are especially brutal—particularly those involving children—and, as it turns out, these rapes are usually perpetrated by men suffering from a diagnosable mental illness. But it is time to recognize that these rapes should neither be the standard against which all reported rapes are judged, nor set apart as qualitatively different from "everyday rape". It may in fact be the case that the most violent and "abnormal" rapes are simply the extreme product of a society which refuses to take rape seriously. When rape results in the victim's death or near-death, we are prepared to condemn it and to find labels which justify severe punishment of the offender. Our failure to take rape seriously at an earlier stage, or to find new labels for the offender, may contribute to the ultimate consequence of the most violent cases. "Everyday rape" should not be dismissed because it fails to exhibit the extreme brutality of those rape-murders which we attribute to the "criminally insane". In allowing rapes of this type to function as the standard of comparison, we simply obscure the real motivation for all rape, the social conditions which explain it, and the true similarities between all cases of rape.

10
victimology: the art of victim blaming

Twenty years ago, Zero Mostel used to do a sketch in which he impersonated a Dixiecrat Senator conducting an investigation of the origins of World War II. At the climax of the sketch, the Senator boomed out in an excruciating mixture of triumph and suspicion, "What was Pearl Harbour DOING in the Pacific?" This is an extreme example of Blaming the Victim. [1]

This anecdote generally brings a round of laughter from those hearing it, but unfortunately, the logic used by Mostel's Senator bears a striking similarity to some of the current academic theories of rape. In the social sciences, victim blaming is becoming an increasingly popular rationalization for criminal and "deviant" behaviour. As one writer has noted, it is usually "cloaked in kindness and concern, and bears all the trappings and statistical furbelows of scientism; it is obscured by a perfumed haze of humanitarianism".[2] Nevertheless, its function is to shore up the *status quo*, for when a social problem can be blamed on its victim, the problem is "solved".

Over the past few years, victim blaming has become institutionalized within the academic world under the guise of victimology.³ The application of victimology to rape paralleled the finding that the rapist is "normal". As less and less of significance was discovered in the psychosexual make-up of the rapist, attention shifted to the victim of rape. This trend was itself the product of two parallel and connected developments in psychology and sociology. As psychology developed from a mentalistic, psychoanalytic account of human action towards a behaviouristic interpretation of individual conduct, sociology was emerging as an independent discipline which sought to explain behaviour in terms of the interactions among people. It offered macroscopic explanations of social phenomena and, of necessity, demanded the adoption of more than one point of view. While behavioural psychology continued to examine the individual, it now concentrated on public, rather than on private facts, since it was concerned to establish that observable behaviour, rather than interior mental entities, were the proper objects of psychological study. Like sociology, behavioural psychology focused on observable behaviour and the dynamics of interpersonal exchange. An individualistic approach never died completely; it continued to flourish within the discipline of psychiatry. Psychiatry itself became and remained the repository of the really hard core cases—the obvious, "diagnosable" psychoses and neuroses.

A concurrent development within psychology was the tendency to reject "old-fashioned and pre-scientific" moralizing in favour of a more "objective" appraisal of human behaviour. Actions which had formerly been regarded as moral aberrations were now regarded as malfunctions of adaptive mechanisms. Criminal behaviour was no longer attributed to moral, psychic defects; nor, indeed, was individual psychic malformation any longer considered to be an adequate explanation for crime. Criminality was now seen to have a social dimension which mentalistic psychology had obscured, and psychiatrists themselves were not long in acknowledging that mental illness was only one reason for criminal behaviour.

Given the general disillusionment with mentalistic explanations of human behaviour, it was only natural that emphasis should shift towards seeing rape as an "interplay"between persons, each of whom shared some degree of responsibility for what happened. The discovery that most rapists were "normal" acted as a catalyst in this change in attitude towards rape, and the apparent normality of the rapist thus served as a springboard for the theory of victimology which portrayed the rape victim as a "participant" in an event for which she was at least partially to blame.

The rapist's seemingly "normal" motivation was taken as an indication that his crime was not very serious, since he was not markedly different from other men, and did not display that gross mental abnormality which one would expect to find in the perpetrator of a grave moral offence. Rape was, after all, a "sexual" offence, and was not committed with the intention of causing harm. Indeed, very little harm could now be seen in most of what came to public attention as alleged rape. It did not display that gross disregard for the lives of others which one would expect to find in an offence carrying such heavy moral and legal sanctions, and many of the alleged victims were not the sort of women that rape laws were designed to protect.

It is hardly surprising, therefore, that social scientists should have begun to view rape as a minor social problem, and one which certainly did not merit its pre-eminent place in the criminal law. The logical corollary of their reasoning was that the women who complain of rape are probably more unbalanced than the men who commit it. In the absence of mental abnormality on the part of the offender, or grave physical harm to the victim, harm exists only in the eye of a woman who feels that her dignity has been offended. Prosecution on such slim justification is, in fact, dangerously close to malicious prosecution, and should subject the complainant to the full disapproval of the law. Thus, the complainant becomes the offender at a rape trial, and the defendant becomes the victim.

social science and self-interest

Victimology provided a new explanation for rape which did not question the old stereotypes, but within the social sciences, there were particular reasons for the ready acceptance of victimological interpretations of rape. These reasons lie in the social scientific method itself, and in the inability of many social scientists to identify personally with the subject of their research. Ryan, for example, explains the thinking of those who blame poor people for their own fate:

First, the question of self-interest, or more accurately, class interest. The typical Victim Blamer is a middle-class person who is doing reasonably well in a material way....Basically he likes the social system pretty much the way it is....On the other hand, he is acutely aware of poverty, racial discrimination, exploitation and deprivation, and moreover, he wants to do something concrete to ameliorate the condition of the poor, the black, and the disadvantaged. This is not an extraneous concern; it is central to his value system to insist on the worth of the individual, the equality of men, and the importance of justice.[4]

In the case of rape, victim blamers can be similarly described. First, there is the question of self-interest, which in this case can more accurately be described as sex interest. The typical victim blamer is a male person who is doing reasonably well in a sexual way (or, at least, enjoys a position of privilege in the sexual exchange). Basically, he likes the sexual system pretty much the way it is. On the other hand, he is acutely aware of rape, sexual exploitation, and the most blatant forms of sexism. This is not an extraneous concern; it is central to his value system to insist on the worth of the individual, the equality of persons, and the importance of justice.

However, the victim blamer is in the rather uncomfortable position of having to seek an explanation for rape within a sexual system which provides the basis for his own sense of masculine identity. Since Western culture has encouraged male dominance in the sexual as well as in the economic and social spheres, it is very difficult for a male theorist to recognize that rape is strikingly similar to the sexual behaviour of men in general—including, perhaps, himself. No researcher has concluded that, since the rapist is a "normal" man, other "normal" men must be potential rapists. But what alternative conclusion can there be? The male researcher finds his escape in victimology. He seeks the problem's cause in the behaviour of its victim, and goes on to persuade himself and the public at large that by changing that behaviour, the problem can be controlled. In this way, the study of victimology becomes the art of victim blaming.

mendelsohn's fallacy:
rape and the eye of the beholder

Beniamin Mendelsohn, one of the pioneers of victimology, very early applied the principles of this "modern science" to the problem of rape.

His study is riddled with sexist assumptions, and his analysis amounts to a virtual denial that men are responsible for rape.

To begin with, Mendelsohn states that rape is all but impossible under normal circumstances:

> I pointed out the possibility of resistance on the part of the woman by the almost inexpugnable position she occupies on account of the topography of the sexual organs in the female body.[5]

This is simply an academic version of "You can't stick a pencil in a moving milk bottle"—a popular theory which has been with us for some time.

However, Mendelsohn does note a few exceptional circumstances in which "authentic" rape may occur. The first is that in which there is "a very great disproportion between the physical strength of the aggressor (or aggressors) and that of the victim"[6] It is not unusual for women to be physically weaker than their assailants, but Mendelsohn does not point this out. Nor does he consider the effect of socialization on a woman's behaviour: if she has been taught from an early age that she is weaker than men, she may submit to rape even though she is, in fact, quite capable of resisting the attack. (Moreover, it may seem wiser to submit than to invite serious injury through further resistance.) Mendelsohn also fails to consider the full social context of rape in his remark that the "familial, authoritative or hierarchical relations existing between the accused and the victim"[7] may lessen her resistance. Men have traditionally exercised authority over women, and no formal relationship need exist between the victim and the offender for that difference in status to have its effect.

But two of the most intriguing reasons which Mendelsohn gives for "authentic rape" are "the volcanic temperament of the victim which may obscure the reasoning faculty" and "the libertine social surroundings of the victim". [8] In some situations, then, women may become so frenzied that they are incapable of rational thought. [9] In others, they are tainted by their surroundings, which are "libertine" (a quaintly old-fashioned, but value-laden term). Mendelsohn's prejudice against women is further revealed in his claim that women often put on a show of "simulated resistance"[10] and in his warning that the "statements of young girls under the age of 15 when giving evidence should be received with greater caution than those of minor boys of the same age".[11]

In general, then, Mendelsohn holds women responsible for rape in almost all circumstances. If women do not provoke rape directly, they fail to resist it when they should, or are indirectly responsible for rape because they are more submissive and less rational creatures than men.

menachem amir and victim-precipitated rape

One of the most comprehensive studies of rape to date is Menachem Amir's *Patterns in Forcible Rape,* which analyzes all rapes reported to the Philadelphia Police Department in 1958 and 1960. This book is one of the principal applications of victimology to rape, and is particularly interesting for its discussion of "victim-precipitated rape". Amir's study at first appears to be carefully "scientific", but its dependence upon traditional preconceptions and value judgments quickly becomes obvious. In defining victim-precipitated rape, Amir refers to

> rape situations in which the victim actually, or so it was deemed, agreed to sexual relations but retracted before the actual act or did not react strongly enough when the suggestion was made by the offender.[12]

Amir found that only 19% of the rapes in his study fit this description, and it is interesting that he should have placed such emphasis on victim-precipitated rape when over four-fifths of his cases did not fall into this category. This, however, becomes a minor problem when one attempts to examine Amir's definition of victim-precipitated rape.

Amir never adequately defines this concept. Beyond the passage quoted above, he limits himself to oblique descriptions of what the term means; for example, he refers to the "sexually charged situations"[13] in which victim-precipitated rape may occur. No further definition is given, nor does Amir appear to think that one is necessary. Despite this inadequate starting point, however, Amir reaches a number of conclusions about victim-precipitated rape: the victim is likely to have a "bad reputation"; alcohol is likely to be present; the initial meeting between the offender and the victim is likely to have taken place in a bar or at a party.[14] Yet these are the same factors which would define a situation as "marred with sexuality"[15] (and therefore rape-precipitating) in the first place. Amir's basic reasoning is circular, since he uses his "conclusions" about victim-precipitated rape to define the phenomenon.

But as it turns out, Amir is prepared to define *any* form of female behaviour as rape-precipitating:

> A woman's behaviour, if passive, may be seen as worthy to suit action, and if active, may be taken as an actual promise of success to one's sexual intentions.[16]

Therefore, a woman cannot win. No matter how she behaves, she may provoke a rape attack. In fact, it is not her behaviour which precipitates rape at all, but the rapist's *interpretation* of her behaviour. Here, Amir reveals both the fallacy and the male bias in his theory. It may well be that 19% (or more) of all women behave in ways which a male bias would perceive as an invitation to rape, but their behaviour is not classified as "rape-precipitating" unless they are actually raped. Amir's unquestioning acceptance of the male perspective is not unique; it is a widespread feature of male-dominated society. But when this general bias is carried into the social sciences, it becomes an academic endorsement of the rapist's point of view, and an excuse for blaming rape upon its victims.

It is also interesting to examine the differences between Amir's study and its apparent model, *Patterns in Criminal Homicide* by Marvin E. Wolfgang.[17] Amir's "victim-precipitated rape" seems to parallel Wolfgang's "victim-precipitated criminal homicide", but there are significant differences of definition between the two concepts. Wolfgang defines his category as

> those criminal homicides in which the victim is a *direct, positive* precipitator in the crime. The role of the victim is characterized by his having been the first in the homicide drama to use physical force directed against his subsequent slayer. The victim-precipitated cases are those in which the victim was the first to show and use a deadly weapon, to strike a blow in an altercation—in short, the first to commence the interplay of resort to physical violence.[18]

Wolfgang is careful to note that "mutual quarrels or wordy altercations"[19] are not sufficient reason for classifying homicide as victim-precipitated, and in general, he rejects situational factors, or actions open to a wide range of interpretations, as grounds for this classification. His concept is in clear contrast to Amir's, in which situational factors, and their interpretation by the offender, form the essence of the definition.

But Amir's analysis of rape has a more basic problem than its flawed methodology. Like other male, middle-class researchers, Amir cannot perceive any connection between rape and the sexual behaviour of men in general. He treats rape as a "deviation", or a function of the "criminal subculture", abstracting it from general patterns of human behaviour. Because he lacks a broad, historical and political understanding of rape, Amir's theory is both narrow and fallacious. By ignoring the coerciveness of "normal" male-female relations, he obscures the true social causes of both rape and social attitudes towards it.

Historically, the complaint of the rape victim has always been suspect and she has been viewed with suspicion and fear. This is an apparent paradox, a seemingly contradictory effect of the historical context out of which the offence of rape developed. But Amir treats effect as cause in positing blameworthy victims as the "cause" of the events about which they complain. He thus relieves theory and practice of responsibility for explaining the apparent contradiction. In no other criminal offence is the complainant viewed as inherently unworthy of belief, but by placing blame upon the victims of rape, Amir neatly rationalizes and justifies the very behaviour which requires explanation.

Nevertheless, many criminologists have used Amir's concept of victim-precipitated rape to explain their own findings. John M. MacDonald is a notable example. In *Rape Offenders and Their Victims*, he suggests that some women "invite rape" [20] or "are rape-prone, as others are accident-prone". [21] MacDonald often comes quite close to realizing the major fallacy in Amir's theory—the confusion of the victim's behaviour with the offender's interpretation of that behaviour. He notes that a victim may be vulnerable to rape when she uses "what *could be interpreted as* indecent language" or makes "what *could be taken as* an invitation to sexual relations" [22] (emphasis ours). However, he never reaches the logical conclusion, that it is the offender's mistaken interpretation which "precipitates" rape, and that it is *rape* which he precipitates.

For MacDonald and other researchers, it is more convenient to retain the concept of victim-precipitated rape than to reassign the locus of responsibility to the offender. Because our society is male-dominated, the male point of view has traditionally been accepted as "correct". Questioning the validity of this perspective would amount to a challenge of the sexual system in which male researchers themselves have a vested interest. Men regard female sexuality as their private property; therefore, they believe that they have the right to decide when and where sexual activity will take place. As an extrapolation from that general belief, the concept of victim-precipitated rape helps to perpetuate a sexual system in which men are sexually dominating and women are expected to be passive and submissive.

victimology and property

The application of victimology to rape maintains the *status quo* in yet another way. By placing specific blame for the crime of rape upon its victim, it justifies the general guilt which women are made to feel if they are raped. A woman is carefully taught that rape is a disgrace, which will cause her to feel great shame. If she doesn't feel it immediately, those around her ensure that she soon will, whether they be parents, priests or psychiatrists. But why should shame, rather than simple anger, be the emotion she is expected to feel?

Rape is a disgrace, because it diminishes a woman's property value. On being raped, a woman becomes "soiled" and her market value drops—no matter how innocent she may be of "complicity" in the event. Because she is a form of property, her rape frustrates the expectations of others, and though blameless, she becomes the instrument through which others' fortunes fall. A woman is made to internalize responsibility for her rape, even though there was nothing she could have done to prevent it, and even though she was not responsible for the expectations which others created around her. But if women were not regarded as private property, as commodities with an exchange value, they would no more be disgraced by rape than by any other form of assault, and would not be asked to feel shame rather than the anger appropriate to an unprovoked attack on one's person.

For the victim, rape is a classic "Catch-22" situation. Even if she is completely innocent of "participation" in the event, and fills all the requirements of respectable womanhood, the rape diminishes her value and causes others to suffer. Men react with anger at having their property damaged, their "legitimate" expectations frustrated, and this anger and frustration is vented on the victim. She is required to prove her innocence, though her ability to do so will, in the end, most often prove fruitless.

The onus has been on the raped woman to prove her innocence from the beginnings of recorded Western history. Victimology simply legitimizes that practice by providing a rationale for it. The assumption has been that if the victim did not intentionally provoke the rape, she may at least have been reckless or negligent in protecting herself. One wonders how far men perceive rape as a subtle form of guerrilla warfare, a weapon which women use to undermine the control which men have over their sexuality. Perhaps this explains the male suspicion that women cry rape out of a desire for revenge (despite the preponderance of evidence that it is men who use rape as a weapon of revenge, against other men).[23] But that question aside, it is clear that men have always been reluctant to see rape victims as the innocent prey of their assailants. This may stem from their reluctance to see other men suffer for an act they might commit themselves, or from the mistrust which ownership of persons always engenders, but their resentment and hostility inevitably centres on the rape victim. It is she who is disgraced and who brings disgrace on others; thus, it is she who must account for herself. What she must prove is that she was the kind of woman who *could* be raped—in other words, that she had a prior property value which should have been respected, and that she actively pursued its protection. If she had no such value, or placed her sexuality in jeopardy, then she has no right to complain of rape, since her assailant was merely appropriating an unclaimed or valueless object for a temporary period, or actualizing a risk she herself created. Why else would information about a woman's sexual history be regarded as relevant evidence in a rape trial? In the eyes of our society, only some women can be raped; for the rest, *tant pis*.

victimology and open territory victims

The popular stereotype of "real rape" is still the attack of a valuable, respectable woman by a moral deviant. Women with only a marginal or disputable value are usually not believed to have been raped at all—but if, technically, they were raped, where is the harm? The typical rapist who attacks these women is simply a man who was unlucky enough to get caught; and if he really is "normal", as the tests have shown him to be, then his actions should not arouse deep moral outrage and indignation. An explanation for rape is still needed, but a convenient justification for the rapist's behaviour can be found in victimology.

It is no accident that the "valueless" women in our society have also been labelled the "precipitators" of rape by the victimologists. Amir, for example, found that the rape precipitators are women with "bad reputations", who drink, and meet men in bars or at parties. And as we have seen, he argues backwards from such descriptions to establish his category of victim-precipitated rape in the first place. The women in this category are also the women we have described as "open territory" victims. Within our system of private, sexual property they are worthless, and do not qualify for the redress or protection of the law. When they become the victims of rape, therefore, the crime must become a non-crime. The attack itself cannot be made to disappear, so the complainant is made responsible for it, and the "victim" vanishes.

Of course, some men believe that all women are "open territory", but most men make a distinction between women who are "off limits" and women who are more acceptable objects of sexual coercion. Those women who are at the bottom of the socio-economic heap in a particular society most often fall into the "open territory" category. In our society, they are the young and the powerless; they may be perceived as "inferior" because of their racial or ethnic backgrounds; they may be prostitutes, or women who fall beyond the boundaries of "respectability" for other reasons; increasingly, they are women who act as if they do not have or need male protectors. Men simply do not perceive themselves to be committing rape when they choose such women as their targets. And society does little to protect such women even when they are the random victims of assault. These women are not valuable to the established system; they may even appear threatening to it. Therefore, their rape is inconsequential, and no less than they deserve for their "antisocial" behaviour. Apparently, then, it is not enough to refuse these women protection from rape. We rationalize their rape by blaming it on them, and by punishing them if they complain.

11
rape
as an assault

If one begins from the naive assumption that rape has legally and historically been an offence against the person, then one can see in rape laws an attempt to articulate a standard of consensual sexuality. The model is one of mutual consent: sexual intercourse is a legally permissible act when it occurs between two consenting adults. The legal offence of rape, then, appears to prohibit sexual intercourse where at least one party does not agree to it. But this interpretation does not square with either the letter of the law, or the treatment of rape within our criminal justice system. First of all, rape is an offence which can only be committed by a male against a female, and against a female who is not his wife. And as we have seen, practically speaking, rape can only be committed against a certain type of female.

Our legal system defines and treats rape as an offence against property, and not as an offence against the person. Rape laws were not designed to protect a woman's right to physical or sexual autonomy, but to preserve male rights of ownership in valuable property, including sexual and reproductive property. And it is the pre-eminent value placed on female sexuality—the quality that makes women most valuable within our system of private property—which accounts for the fact that rape has historically been defined as a "sexual offence". As they now stand, our laws define rape from the male point of view, and describe what men think is wrong with it.

The predominance of the male perspective is also responsible for the deeply-rooted belief that rape is a disgrace to its victim. Rape victims are only "credible" if they display a high degree of emotional distress and feel shamed and guilty about what has happened to them. Such feelings are appropriate to a woman who has accepted the evaluation of herself as a primarily sexual being, whose main worth lies in her potential for exclusive ownership. But if her sexuality were not so highly prized by men (and therefore by herself), such feelings would be neither appropriate nor expected.

It is men, and not women, who have defined rape as the worst thing that can happen to a woman. For a man to have his exclusive sexual property defiled by an intruder is one of the worst things that can happen to *him*, but it most assuredly is not the worst thing that can happen to a woman, even though it frequently verges on this because of its accompanying risk. What woman would not rather have a penis inserted in her vagina, even against her will, than suffer death or mutilation? Women accept the judgment that rape is a disgrace because they, too, have been brainwashed into placing pre-eminent value on their sexuality, and because they know from experience that rape will, in fact, lead to their social and personal devaluation.

sexual property and sexual harm

Men have defined rape as a sexual offence because it is an attack on their sexual property. One of the worst consequences of this definition is that it leaves no harm to be punished unless a "valuable" woman is physically damaged by the rape attack.[1] If no economic harm is done, or if this harm is very minimal, there appears to be no theoretical basis for treating rape as a legal offence or for punishing the rapist. The rapist commits a wrongful act because he damages or "steals" another's property; his crime is sexual because the property stolen is sexual. But when the victim does not belong to somebody else, or possess qualities which make her potentially valuable, then her rape cannot be perceived as wrong.

The denial of any other harm in the act of rape is furthered by an ambiguous use of the term "sexual offence". As used above, the label "sexual offence" is exactly correct. It indicates the source of women's property value to men, and the harm which men suffer when that property is attacked. But in common usage, "sexual offence" takes on a second meaning which conveniently blurs the first. This interpretation emphasizes the sexual nature of the act itself, and suggests that rape is primarily a sexual encounter between a man and a woman, rather than a form of physical assault.

To view rape in this way is to accept the rapist's claim that rape is nothing other than an expression of normal sexual desire. As he sees it, the object of the encounter is merely sexual intercourse, which in itself is a source of pleasure. If any harm is done, it is only incidental to the rapist's real intention, which is to give and to receive pleasure. The concept of rape as a purely sexual offence obscures even the real economic harm suffered by the victim and her owner, but if the victim is not devalued by the attack, then this mystification of rape allows the judicial system to deny her any right of redress.

what makes sexual intercourse rape?

Because rape is a crime against property, its key legal element is the status and character of the rape victim; that is, the judgment of wrong-doing depends upon the nature of the property in question. The law only prohibits forcible sexual intercourse if it is committed against a particular type of object—namely, a woman with an actual or potential property value, to which the rapist has no legitimate claim. Otherwise, the act is permissible, even if characterized by physical coercion.

The main issue to be decided in law is whether a man's actual or potential property rights have been violated by the rapist. If they have not, then the act in question did not cause the type of harm which rape laws were meant to prohibit. Unless the rape constitutes such a violation of rights or results in serious physical harm to the victim, there is no legal wrong to be redressed. This is why a man may force sexual intercourse upon his wife without being accused of rape. He is her proper owner, and may use her sexuality as he sees fit. But if he were to force the same act upon another man's wife, he would then be guilty of rape.

coercion, submission and consent

After the character of the victim, the second most important ingre-
dient of the offence of rape is the victim's lack of consent. Within the
framework of the criminal law, it is assumed that rape differs from
other acts of sexual intercourse only in that a certain mental element is
missing on the part of one of its participants. It must be proved that the
victim did not consent to sexual intercourse, or if she did, that her
consent was extorted through the use or threat of physical violence.
What makes sexual intercourse rape is not the offender's use or threat
of physical force, but proof that a "rapable" female did not consent to
the act in question.

Evidence of physical coercion does not lead automatically to the
presumption that the victim did not "consent" to the act; lack of consent must be proved separately. The law thus holds the rather odd
view that a rape victim can genuinely consent to sexual intercourse
even if the threat or reality of physical violence is used to prevent her
resistance. Worse, the absence of consent must be supported by tangible evidence; it will rarely be inferred from the victim's testimony that
she simply said "no". Instead, lack of consent must be inferred from
evidence that the victim actively resisted the attack and attempted to
prevent sexual intercourse from occurring, regardless of the risk she
ran in doing so. If there is no such evidence, then her "consent" will be
assumed. Saying "no" is apparently not enough, even in the face of
physical violence.

Since the victim's consent can be used as a defence to the charge of
rape, the victim must resist her attacker to the utmost of her
capabilities if her later testimony concerning lack of consent is to appear credible. But if she engages in prolonged resistance, she may invite further abuse, serious injury, or even death. A victim who can
remain level-headed during an attack may realize that it is rational to
submit to rape in such circumstances. This is a good deal easier said
than done, and if accomplished it is a mark not of consent, but of the
triumph of reason. Most victims resist their attackers to some degree;
it is a natural physical response to try to avoid physical abuse. But the
absence of resistance is certainly not an indication of consent.

If more victims of assault—rape and otherwise—could control
their physical reactions to attack, they would suffer far less physical
harm. This is a fact which the law recognizes by classifying as an assault not only completed forms of physical interference, but attempt-

ed forms of such interference and actual interference accomplished by means of verbal or other threats. Only in the rape situation does the law construe the absence of resistance as nullifying the occurrence of an offence. The law does not perceive the failure to resist forcible sexual intercourse as a rational judgment of how best to minimize risk, but as conscious or unconscious "consent" to the act in question —even where it was accomplished through the use or threat of physical force.

Clearly, what the law calls "consent" should actually be termed "submission". But if you submit to rape, then—according to the law—you have "consented", and the onus is on you to prove that the threat of abuse, or the violence already suffered, justified that "consent". While the legal definition specifies that rape occurs where the victim does not consent to the act, or where her consent "is extorted by threats or fear of bodily harm", practically speaking this means that unless the victim did resist, and can corroborate her resistance with material evidence, her lack of consent will not be believed, no matter what happened during the rape attack. If she admits that she did "consent" (that is, submit) in the face of violence, then she must prove that this violence was severe enough to justify her failure to resist. In court, whether she argues that she did not consent, or that she submitted to avoid risk and injury, the legal issue will be the same: did she resist? And unless she can prove that the risk was very great indeed, her testimony as to the non-consensual nature of the act will not be credible. She must prove that she acted reasonably in submitting to the risk created by the offender's behaviour. But no matter what approach is taken by the prosecution, the fact of physical coercion, and the victim's lack of consent, are matters which must be proved by the *victim*, even though it was the accused who created the risk.

The law has said that lack of consent is the distinguishing feature of rape, but this is surely to miss the obvious. It is not the absence of consent, but the presence of physical coercion, which makes rape fundamentally different from "normal" acts of sexual intercourse. In a situation where a woman has no real choice, the question of her consent becomes patently irrelevant.

Sexual intercourse is the only form of social transaction which is not automatically redefined by the presence of physical coercion. All exchanges of money between one person and another are monetary in nature, but an exchange of money to which the owner freely consents is referred to as a "gift", whereas an exchange of money which the recipient effects through physical coercion is referred to as a "theft". And it is assumed that where the recipient used or threatened physical force, the donor did not consent to the act in question. Gifts and thefts are both monetary transactions, but it is the differences, rather than the similarities, between them which are thought to be important —important enough to be marked by a verbal distinction.

In the case of monetary exchanges, the mere presence of physical coercion negates any presumption of consent on the part of the giver and hence makes the issue of consent *prima facie* irrelevant. Why is this not also the rule with physically coerced acts of sexual intercourse? Only in the case of sexual transactions do we refuse to acknowledge that the relevant issue is the offender's behaviour rather than the victim's state of mind. In rape, as in theft, the use or threat of physical force ought to negate any presumption of consent on the victim's part.

The point we wish to establish here is that sexual intercourse characterized by the use or threat of violence is not "sexual intercourse" at all, where we are taking "sexual intercourse" to mean "consensual sexual relations"; it is so vastly different from the latter that it should only be referred to as "rape". And if "rape" is then understood to mean "sexual intercourse accomplished through the use or threat of physical force", then correctly describing an act as "rape" allows no room for the issue of consent to arise in the way it traditionally has.

The issue underlying the verbal problem here must be clearly understood, because of its practical consequences for rape victims. Except in the case of rape, the law has recognized and clearly articulated the basic principle that an act characterized by the presence of physical coercion is fundamentally different from the same act occurring in circumstances which are not physically coercive. This basic principle should also apply to sexual intercourse. Rape should be prohibited because it is characterized by physical coercion, and the absence of consent should be a secondary issue.

The presence of physical coercion should negate any presumption that the victim consented to the act; or else, we should reverse our practices elsewhere, and make the victims of theft, for example, prove that they didn't consent to the forcible taking of their money! In court, lack of consent would be, as elsewhere, a rebuttable presumption, and the defence would always have an opportunity to show that the victim did consent to the act, despite the presence of physical coercion. But the burden of proof would shift from the prosecution to the defence. Instead of requiring proof of the victim's *lack* of consent, the courts would require the defence to rebut the presumption that this consent was absent. The main task of the prosecution would then be to prove that the accused used or threatened physical violence in order to force sexual intercourse upon his victim.

And if the consent of the victim is to be an allowable defence, though one which requires the defendant to prove that the victim did consent to sexual intercourse despite his use or threat of violence, then the notion of "consent" must be sharply differentiated from "submission". Submission in response to the risk of injury is not consent, and it must be made absolutely clear that consent may not be inferred from lack of resistance. If a person is threatened with, or subjected to physical coercion to prevent her from resisting a sexual act, then she in no sense "consents" to the act done; no relevant sense of "consent" may be inferred from her failure to resist or otherwise attempt to thwart the act being forced upon her. The same standards which apply to other acts characterized by the threat or reality of physical coercion should also apply to acts of sexual intercourse.

The law refuses to recognize the coerciveness of many rape situations because it reflects, and is rooted in, the historical assumption that women do not have the right to be sexually self-determining. A woman does not have the right to control her own sexual organs: they must either be the exclusive property of one man, or the common property of all men. And in the rape situation, a woman must choose between these two options. If she values her sexuality more than her life, we will punish acts in which she defends her sexuality to the point of death. But short of that, she can expect no redress from the law. By failing to resist at all costs and against all odds, she has forfeited her right to protection and declared herself to be common property; therefore, she has no right to resist a rape attack at all, and if she is hurt through her resistance, she is responsible for bringing injury upon herself. Either she must see her sexual organs as more important than anything else, even her life, or we will not punish those who attack her sexual organs.

This is obviously the paradigm case of "damned if you do, damned if you don't". Because our legal and social structures perpetuate the belief that women are forms of private property, whose value consists in their sexual and reproductive functions, women are expected to share that belief and to value their sexuality above all else. Thus, women ought to be prepared to die in its defence. If they do, their assailants will be punished whether or not they intended this result; but if women do not die in defence of their sexuality, and have not suffered grave physical injury, they do not deserve redress because their sexual integrity is not properly a matter for their own autonomous control. If they still have a sexual value for someone, then no harm has been done. And since no harm was intended, there is no basis for serious punishment.

This is very far from the experience and perspective of rape victims. Because women do not accept the view that they are common sexual property, and that their sexual organs are not parts of their bodies which deserve the same protection as other parts of their bodies, they continue to experience rape as a potentially dangerous assault on their physical persons. But the message which society and the law convey to women is clear and unequivocal. Despite the fact that every rape is performed by the offender and experienced by the victim as a potentially life-threatening assault, it is not unless death or near-death results that society is prepared to view rape as essentially assaultive in nature, and to punish it as such.

the female perspective: rape as an assault

In suggesting that the presence of physical coercion, rather than the absence of consent, should be the central feature of the offence of rape, we are saying that our rape laws should reflect the perspective of women—the victims of rape. For women, the presence of physical coercion defines the nature of the act. They experience rape as an *assault*, as an unprovoked attack on their physical person, and as a transgression of their assumed right to the exclusive ownership and control of their own bodies.

A primary freedom guaranteed by virtually all societies is freedom from unwarranted physical attack and coercion by others. This is the most basic form of security and represents the most fundamental justification for the imposition of legal sanctions. In the act of rape, a male forces a female to submit to his physical desires, and uses her body against her will. This act is experienced by the rape victim as a denial of her physical autonomy, and she senses it to be a violation of the central moral and legal rights which society has an obligation to protect. To her, the fact that this assault was directed against her sexual organs is—at least at the time—irrelevant. Rape is a physical attack on her person, and she believes she has the right to be protected from such attacks. This follows from her belief that she is a fully human person, and entitled to all the protections given to persons under the law. Since she knows that the right to exclusive control over one's own body, and to freedom from unprovoked physical interference by others, are two of the fundamental rights guaranteed to persons under the law, she quite justifiably expects redress when she is raped. Imagine her surprise when she discovers that, because this assault was directed against her sexual organs, as opposed to some other part of her body, it has been removed from the category of assault and reclassified as a "sexual offence", which does not carry the same rights of redress as an "assault".

It certainly comes as a shock to most women to learn that attacks on their sexual organs which do not result in physical injury are not illegitimate and will not lead to punishment of their assailants. So far as women are concerned, their sexual organs are no less, and no different, a part of their person than their heads, eyes and limbs; their personhood is constituted as much by the integrity of their sexual organs as by the integrity of their other bodily parts. But the rape event catapults them into fast awareness that their sexual organs are, legally and socially speaking, not parts of their autonomous person. The inference is clear: women do not have the right to sexual autonomy.

This is sensed as totally arbitrary—not only because it is totally arbitrary to conceptualize female sexual organs as being governed by a different legal framework than that which governs other bodily parts—but for the further reason that rape is always experienced as a potentially *life-threatening* situation.[2] Since sexual organs are just parts of the body, an attack on the sexual organs is as threatening to life and health as an unprovoked attack on any of the other bodily parts. Rape is thus experienced by the victim as an unprovoked physical assault which endangers her life. Nevertheless, the only assaults directed against sexual organs that society is fully prepared to punish are those which do, in fact, result in serious injury, mutilation or death. Those which do not have such drastic results are not perceived as life-threatening because they are seen as *sexual* acts—acts intended not to harm, but to please.

Seeing rape only as a sexual act obscures both its assaultive nature, and its potential risk to life. When such risk materializes, when death or near-death actually results, then we are prepared to punish rape. But with a semantic sleight of hand, these acts are at once reinstated as assaults and classified as "homicide" or "attempted homicide". The fact that these crimes were attacks on sexual organs becomes irrelevant, and indeed invisible.

Any physical attack is a potential risk to life and an attack on the sexual organs is as dangerous as any other form of assault. But this fact is obscured by the common assumption that rapists intend no harm to their victims. The point, however, is that harm occurs whether intended or not, and that this harm should be punished, whether intended or not. The same standards which apply to assaults against other parts of the body should also apply to attacks against the sexual organs.

Moreover, the physical risk which accompanies rape is often underestimated. There is a widespread belief that very few rapes lead to murder, but this assumption appears to be totally unsupported by statistical evidence. Certainly, such a conclusion cannot be derived from an analysis of rape cases, because cases tried as rapes are cases in which death did not result. Murder is simply the worst outcome of assault, and the classification of rape as a purely "sexual" offence disguises its connections with other assaultive crimes.

future perspectives: rape and the creation of risk

It is thus our belief that rape must be removed from the category of sexual offences and reclassified as an assault. Rape is merely one form of unprovoked attack on the physical person, whether it is perpetrated by a male or a female, on a male or a female. As such, it need be subject to none of the "special" rules which currently apply to the offence of rape, and which are rooted in the false assumption that rape is not an assaultive crime but a sexual act done with the wrong woman.

As with other assaults, the severity of the punishment should be decided in accordance with the degree of actual harm inflicted on the victim, the potential risk to the victim created by the actual violence used or threatened, and the potential risk to other members of society created by the particular offender. And, at least during a temporary transitional phase, punishments should be meted out with the clear knowledge that, since many women do accept the view of themselves as having a value based primarily on their sexuality, rape must be punished according to the degree of damage felt to have been done by the victim. A woman who strongly identifies with traditional concepts of women's status in our society deserves redress for injuries done to her as a consequence of accepting those concepts, whether or not she suffers any very grave or permanent physical damage.

While this may be seen as a form of reverse discrimination, it represents no great departure from established legal principles. In a civil assault and battery action, the assailant cannot claim less responsibility for the damage he actually inflicts upon his victim on the grounds that his victim suffered from a pre-existing condition which rendered him more liable to serious injury than someone else. This is known as the "glass-jaw" principle, and it can be roughly formulated as "you take your victim as you find him". If a person assaults a man with a particularly fragile jaw, who therefore suffers much more damage than he would have without that prior condition, that does not mitigate blame for his assailant. If you assault someone, you are responsible for the damage you cause, whether or not it was intended and whether or not you could, or did, foresee it. This should also be the case in a rape assault. If the victim of such an attack is a woman who feels that her value as a person has been seriously reduced by the act, then those feelings must be respected and reflected in the sentence awarded the offender, whether or not she suffered any serious physical injury. Having arranged all of our legal and social structures so that women will view themselves as valuable pieces of sexual property, with a value determined by their sexual and reproductive function, the least we can do is redress injuries done to them when they accept that framework of values and assumptions.

But the basic principles which must be accepted and given a determinate legal shape, are that attacks on one's sexual organs are as assaultive, and hence as potentially dangerous to life, as assaults on any other part of the body; that punishment should in no way be a direct function either of the degree of physical harm actually inflicted or of the harm intended; and, that "consent" is not logically equivalent to "submission" and may not be inferred from the rape victim's failure to resist. The point is that, as an assault, rape always creates a *potential* risk to life, and it is an assessment of that risk which ought to be reflected in the punishment for rape. And of course, as in all such judgments, the assessment of potential risk must be made up of both subjective and objective components. If a rapist threatens his victim with death, and tells her that he has a knife, it is reasonable for her to believe that the potential risk is grave whether or not it turns out that he actually did have a knife, and whether or not he intended to make good his threat. If it was reasonable for her to believe that a grave risk existed, then he deserves to be punished for creating that risk. It must be made absolutely clear, both in the law and in society at large, that this form of physical assault will not be tolerated any more than any other, and that anyone guilty of rape is liable for punishment whether or not he intended harm to the victim, and whether or not he in fact produced any physical harm. The physically coerced use of another person's body is punishable in its own right, quite apart from the question of actual harm intended or produced. In this, as in any other form of assault, the word of the victim should be as inherently credible as the word of the accused, and no evidence concerning her past or present sexual experiences should be considered in any way relevant to establishing her *prima facie* credibility regarding the event in question.

Only if these changes are made, can women gain the full and basic protections afforded to persons under the law and undermine the basic concept of women as forms of private property with an essentially sexual value. We must establish and firmly entrench the principle that sexual autonomy is as much a right of women as it is of men, and one which is included within that notion of the autonomy of persons which is among our most fundamental legal and social principles. Like other forms of physical assault, rape must be defined and treated as an offence against the person, and not as an offence against property.

12
freedom
from rape

In chapter 1 we began our discussion of the problem of rape in terms of two widely-held attitudes towards rape, the rape victim, and the rape offender. We pointed out that, on the one hand, rape is regarded as the primal act of violence, perpetrated against the purest of the pure by someone who is the symbolic embodiment of evil. On the other hand, what is called "rape" is often regarded as nothing more than a misunderstanding, a simple act of sexual intercourse between two persons with diverging perceptions—the male believing that his behaviour was justifiable given the actions of the female, and she believing that what he did was wrong because she did not fully consent to the act, whatever may have transpired before it. That such attitudes are contradictory seems obvious, but what is less obvious are the connections between them which would explain the contradiction.

This contradiction clearly demonstrates deep ambiguity around the very fundamental question, "What is rape?" and it is this basic question that we hope to have answered in the course of this book. We believed that this could best be done by tracing the development of apparently contradictory beliefs about rape in order to show that they have a common root, a shared history, out of which the modern duality arises. The central fact which explains both sets of attitudes is the historical status of women as forms of private property. The primary qualities which made women desirable as appropriable, marriageable properties were their sexual and reproductive capacities, and the economic assets which they would bring with them into marriage. All men had an interest in defending the chastity of women of property, since these were the kind of women all men desired as marriage partners. The "goodness" of women was defined in terms of their desirability as objects of an exclusive sexual relationship; a "good" woman, therefore, was a woman who resisted all temptation to squander her limited resources and who fought to preserve her assets for the man who could rightfully lay claim to them.

The possibility that such a woman could be violated, her efforts notwithstanding, was a constant threat to a system which demanded virginity prior to marriage, and unbending fidelity after it. The worst thing that could happen to a man was the destruction of sexual property under his control, since it rendered his daughters less desirable as marriageable properties and destroyed his wife's status as sexual property to which he had exclusive access. All men, regardless of their own propertied status, had an interest in preserving the women under their ownership in the condition best suited to advance their own interests. And "real rape", the violation of a virgin or chaste wife, was therefore regarded by them as a heinous and criminal act, perpetrated by someone who refused to accept the established structures. Men who refused to abide by the rules and institutions determining rights of appropriation and ownership of women were regarded as outcasts and traitors. This, then, was the genesis of one set of prevalent attitudes towards rape. The act was, and is, seen as deeply subversive, since it undermines the structures necessary to the continuation of a system of private property under the exclusive control of males. It specifies the victim as one who is either vigorously virginal or chastely monogamous, and it specifies the offender as one who is a social outcast and misfit.

However, since women's sexual and reproductive capacities were the qualities which men bargained and paid for, female sexuality became a commodity, and like any other commodity it had various price tags. It was thus inevitable that valuable female sexual property would on occasion be stolen, since not all men had equal access to the most desirable women. Desirable women, so defined, created a constant temptation. But all women were a temptation, precisely because each woman had to be fitted into a system of guaranteed, exclusive, sexual and reproductive access. Just as women were regarded and socialized to be the property of only one man, so men were socialized to regard individual women as the property of other men, at least until they themselves purchased the rights of access to one (or more) women who would be "theirs". From the outset, therefore, men were forced to regard women as a challenge, not only as the preferred outlets for their sexual desires, but as either potentially appropriable objects of exclusive ownership, or the valued property of someone else. Men were, of course, socialized to respect the property rights of other men, and the very notion of "property rights" in female sexuality gave rise to the possibility that other men could be cheated out of what was rightfully theirs. Thus, sexual intercourse with a woman who was not one's "own" offered endless possibilities for one-upmanship and revenge.

Fundamental to the concept of rape as revenge was acceptance of the premise that, in having sexual intercourse with a woman to whom one had no legal access, one was not violating *her* rights, but the rights of the man who owned her. Rape was a way of cheating or humiliating another man. From the belief that a woman did not own her sexual and reproductive capacities, it followed that a man did not do anything wrong to *her* in the act of forcible intercourse. This logic made it possible for men to view the apparently non-consenting woman as acting not in terms of her own desires but purely out of respect for her actual or potential owner. The "she said no but meant yes" syndrome so commonly heard from rapists and other normal men is rooted in the awareness that women sometimes do say "no" out of fear or respect for the men who own them, rather than from a genuine desire not to have intercourse. Thus, a man who acts contrary to the express wishes of the victim can always rationalize his behaviour, and hers, by maintaining that she really did want sexual relations with him but knew that she would be violating someone else's rights if she acted in accordance with her own real desires.

This, then, explains the other set of attitudes characteristically found in connection with rape, attitudes which are grounded in the conviction that women really do want sexual intercourse even when they say they do not. This belief is reinforced by many women's frank admission that they would agree to intercourse were it not for the fact that their fathers, boyfriends or husbands would kill them if they found out. Rape, then, occurs against the consent of the female in a technical sense, but her lack of consent is seen to be compromised, flowing not from her lack of desire, but from her fear of the consequences.

All of the arguments based on enticement and provocation are rooted in men's belief that if a woman appears provocative and enticing to them, then she really does desire sexual contact with them but cannot admit it or act accordingly. Such an expression of desire would be an exercise of rights of sexual autonomy which women do not in fact have. And the fear of false accusation rests on these assumptions as well, since a false rape charge can be seen as a protective strategy used by women who fear reprisals from those who own them. A woman cannot admit that she wants sexual intercourse with a man who does not own her, because that admission would be a violation of either her trustee relationship to her own sexuality, or of her owner's property rights. And it is public awareness of these assumptions which has led to viewing rape merely as a form of sexual intercourse which is illegal because conducted between the wrong parties. It involves a victim who is at least partially to blame, because she herself has committed a wrong in having desires which run counter to the rights of others, and it involves a normal male who at best acted on the expectations created by the victim's behaviour, or at worst simply failed to recognize her genuine lack of consent.

Since the status of women as private, sexual and reproductive property has created the problem of rape as we know it, it seems obvious to us that the problem cannot be resolved until women are no longer accorded that status but are regarded as having the right to sexual and reproductive autonomy. Historically, rape has been sexual intercourse with a woman to whom a male has no legitimate rights of sexual access; it is punishable only if perpetrated against a woman who is owned by another man, and only if there is tangible and material proof that the woman resisted the attack. Failure to resist is taken as evidence that the woman really did desire sexual contact even though she may have said "no", for in saying "no", she is thought to be paying mere lip service to the duties imposed on her by her status as the sexual and reproductive property of another.

It is the belief—held by both men and women—that women do not have the right to sexual and reproductive autonomy, which also explains the persistent ambiguity and confusion surrounding the relation and differences between rape and seduction. Seduction involves persuading a woman to act according to her own desires and contrary to the duties imposed on her, while rape is a violation of her explicit desire to avoid sexual intercourse with anyone lacking legal rights of access. The traditional concept of rape presupposes either that women who are "real" rape victims have no sexual desires of their own, or that their own desires are completely merged with the desire to restrict their sexual relations to the men who own them. What is called rape, then, is like other forms of coercive sexuality, simply the by-product of a system of institutionalized inequalities in which females have the status of forms of private property and lack rights to sexual and reproductive autonomy.

How we think about ourselves, how we educate and socialize ourselves, and how we regulate our actions through institutions of social control, are all determined to a large extent by the assumptions and implications which follow from the major premise that women are among the forms of private property owned and controlled by men. It would be a mistake to believe, however, that "sexism" is a function of the attitudes and beliefs of individual males or even of males considered as a class or as a group. Sexism is a result of structure. That structure itself rests on a sexist assumption, of course, namely that there is a "natural" inequality of the sexes and that men are "superior". But it is the continuation of structures which were erected on that assumption, which give it a legal and social shape, which are responsible for producing the sexist attitudes and practices so obvious to us today. Thus, the blame for these attitudes and practices should not be laid at the feet of men, either collectively or individually. Men today are as incapable of avoiding the effects of these structures as women are. Even men who want genuinely egalitarian relationships with women find that this is not possible given the institutions, structures and practices of our society; and when men come to realize this, they also realize why women have the fears they do, and why these structures are as destructive to men as to women.

Our approach is not in any way anti-male, though it is strongly opposed to sexism, and to any social system erected on the assumption of inequality between kinds of persons such that power and authority accrue only to a pre-selected subset. Within the theoretical framework we are developing we do not posit—indeed, we specifically reject —any view which would trace the causes of our present difficulties to any "inherent" differences between the sexes, such as the presence of greater aggressiveness in the male, or the greater tendency of females to be nurturing and generative. Sexism is not the product of an inherent male desire to dominate women. Though our society is male dominated, male domination cannot be explained by the theory that each and every man wants to dominate women, or by the statement that we are simply socialized into different and unequal roles. Our society is characterized by institutions and practices (and the socialization processes necessary to support them), which consistently and systematically ensure that only men rise to positions of power and authority in the public world, while women remain at home, in the private sphere, under the legal ownership and control of their husbands. Socialization processes prepare us for structurally predetermined positions, but do not by themselves create those positions. Individual men alive and well and living in Canada today, are no more responsible for creating those institutions and practices than are women, and men are also subject to the arbitrary limitation of their choices. Individually, men are as incapable of changing their position as are women; their sexuality and social roles are as clearly fixed. No amount of resocialization of individuals, either male or female, will alter the structure which creates unequal status, and to believe that it does, or can, is a dangerous illusion. Individual men who choose not to be "sexist" are wonderful, but their choice does not, in any way, disturb the structure which creates an advantaged position for them whether they want it or not. Whether reflected in rape laws or marriage and matrimonial property laws, sexism is structural; it is not simply the result of inherent biological or psychological differences between the sexes, or of superficial socialization processes.

This is not to deny, however, that brute force was and is used by men to brutalize women into submission. All unequal power relationships must, in the end, rely on the threat or reality of violence to maintain themselves. This is true whether the power relationship exists between males and females, between white males and black males, or between the rich industrialized nations of the West and the poor and developing countries of the Third World. And it is also true whether or not the use or threat of violence is manifested by the system as a whole, or solely by individuals. The "colonial mentality" which licensed individual colonialists to oppress and brutalize the individual members of the colonized race, could not have existed without the support of the armed imperialist forces which established and maintained the imperialist/colonized relationship.

It is also true that such structured inequalities will always be bolstered by reference to spurious "facts" which are used to justify the inequalities legally created and enforced. Thus, the unequal legal status of men and women was justified on the grounds that women were weaker than men, that men were rational and reflective, that women were emotional and dominated by their bodily sensations and functions. These were the kinds of claims made to defend the more generalized assumption that there was a "natural" inequality between the sexes, and that women were inferior to men. In turn, this assumption was used to explain and justify the fact that women were regarded, and legally regulated, as forms of private property under the ownership and control of individual men. These beliefs all form part of the *ideology* of male supremacy, and they are reflected in the various socialization processes which prepare us for and maintain us in the roles which our social structures have decreed to be our destiny. But ideology must not be confused with function; inequality in the status of men and women was created to fulfill a specific societal need at a determinate and decisive point in history. Though ideology is used to justify the allocation of unequal status, it is identical neither to the status nor to the need which created it.

Ideology is powerful in its own right, of course, and may outlive the functions and inequalities of status which it serves to justify. A belief in the natural superiority of men has clearly outlived both the specific societal need it was used to justify and the legal status of women which accommodated that need. But it remains obvious that the primary mode of social change is structural change; ideology may lag behind, but without the structures it was meant to support, it becomes much less dangerous. Thus, as we see it, the way to attack sexism in our society is to undermine and destroy the structures which preserve the unequal legal status of men and women; it is not to concentrate on exposing the falsity of its supporting ideology. Ideas are powerless without implementation; therefore, the primary targets of attack should be the structures and institutions which create and maintain inequality.

But once women recognize the nature of their historical status, and the denial of their right to sexual and reproductive autonomy, the history of women's struggles emerges much more clearly as having a consistent and persistent objective. It is the history of a battle to change the legal and social status of women from that of forms of private property to that of persons capable of exercising property rights historically reserved to the male. Over time, women have gradually been gaining, or regaining, control over aspects of their persons and their lives by acquiring rights of ownership to the various goods and benefits which were formerly reserved exclusively to the ownership of men. The right to vote and otherwise participate in the political process, the right to wages paid for productive labour, the right to be educated, and the right to control reproduction, are all rights which have progressively eroded our status as forms of private property under the exclusive control of individual men. Each of these victories has been yet another nail in the coffin of institutionalized sexual inequality, and each has greater significance when viewed in this way, since the cumulative effect of such changes has been, in fact, to transform women's legal and social status and to give them a position of equality within the social, legal and economic structure.

Today we stand on the threshold of becoming full legal persons. As legal persons, women, like men, will be in a position to acquire forms of private property; they will no longer be objects of private property to be appropriated and owned by others. But we are not there yet. It is clear from the continued existence of prejudicial laws governing rape, abortion, and the distribution of matrimonial property, and from the continued absence of adequate equal pay legislation, that women have not yet fully emerged from their status as objects, rather than subjects of property rights. Not until all of these fights have been won will women truly be free persons capable of living autonomous lives.

Many women find it difficult to grasp and accept the fact that in many key areas of their lives, they do not have rights of ownership and, hence, control over the things and legal relations which in fact determine the nature of their existence. Women do not like to see themselves as the objects of private ownership. But our dislike of that degrading status should not blind us to its historical reality. To deny it is also to miss seeing how far we have come. Not until there is full recognition and acknowledgment of that fact, can we begin to understand the significance of our own history, and to shape our own futures. We cannot even begin to understand ourselves, our world, and the complementary self-concept and history of men and their world, until we grasp that fact in its full depth. We now stand mid-way between being forms of private property and potential subjects of private property; this can indeed serve as a signal that the battle is not in vain, but it must not obscure the fact and significance of our historical roots within a structure of male-controlled, private property. The primary determinant of existing social relations is private property, and the primary determinant of the social relations between the sexes is the status of women as forms of that private property under the exclusive ownership and control of men.

So far as the problem of rape is concerned, new approaches must be based on the assumption that rape is a violation of every woman's right to sexual autonomy, and wrong because it is an unjustified interference with her physical person, no different in kind from any other form of physical interference. It is not until women begin to demand that rape be regarded and treated in this way, that the problem as we know it can be eliminated. So long as we persist in the view that rape is wrong because it is an attack on female sexuality we can do nothing to effect fundamental change. Women must begin to reject those socialization processes which teach them to place undue emphasis on their sexuality as their primary source of value. From any rational perspective, rape is not the worst thing that can happen to a woman. A sexual attack is, in itself, neither better nor worse than any other kind of attack. But if those aspects of rape which do create a risk to the life and well-being of the victim were stressed, rather than her alleged "character", or the sexual nature of the offence, then we might be able to prevent the worst assaultive outcomes of such attacks. To treat rape as a sexual offence simply because it involves a penis and a valuable vagina, only reinforces the connections between women as property and women's sexuality as the source of their property value. Existing rape laws force us to accept such attitudes if we wish to gain redress for our injuries, but it guarantees redress only if we are prepared to die in defence of what we have been socialized to accept as our most valued possession.

The two principles, that present rape laws are essentially property laws dependent on concepts of women as sexual property, and that rape should be legally and socially treated as only one form of assault, are the two guiding threads throughout the preceding discussion. It is our belief that many of the errors in past approaches to rape, both popular and academic, have stemmed from a fundamental failure to understand rape within our particular historical, legal, social, and economic context. Once rape is seen in this way, much that is puzzling and apparently contradictory disappears, and avenues towards a solution appear open.

The desire to argue for a new legal definition of rape, and to undermine further the unequal legal status of men and women, was the perspective out of which the present book was undertaken. It was not long before we concluded that the state of past rape research was a shambles. The theory of victimology and its derivative corollaries appeared to function as an elaborate justification for the *status quo*; they simply rationalized the rapist's behaviour and directed attention away from the real problem. Victimology justified the facts which many feminists found disturbing: that much of what women believed to be rape was unreported, that much reported rape was held to be unfounded, that few rape convictions were achieved, and that sentences for convicted rapists were well below the maximum penalties. The acknowledgment that all of these facts deserved serious attention, and are indicators of severe malfunctions in the criminal justice system, would have entailed massive changes in public attitudes, police and court procedures, legislative provisions, and therapeutic approaches to the treatment of convicted offenders.

Acknowledgment of the need for changes of such magnitude would have demanded the reassessment of accepted "theory", and of the relation between that theory and the social circumstances in which it is embedded. Understandably, massive conceptual and procedural upheaval is rarely perceived as the option of first choice, but it is occasionally unavoidable. And the desire to avoid change does not justify the steps taken to conceal its necessity. Fortunately, such attempts at concealment are generally not successful for long. Despite the fact that the theory of victimology and its derivative and supportive assumptions served a structural need in justifying the *status quo*, and in providing a diversionary option to reform, they could neither obliterate the causes of the problems they attempted to justify, nor successfully quell the increasing demand for extensive reforms and reappraisals. Victimology served a functional need at a time when both the public and the professionals were unwilling to question basic assumptions about the sexes, and about the extent to which sexual inequality was a structural rather than a merely attitudinal characteristic of contemporary society. But it became increasingly dysfunctional with increasing knowledge of the extent to which sexual inequality is deeply structural.

Thus, in presenting the first major, empirical study of rape in Canada, we felt an urgent responsibility to do more than simply present the bare "facts". Indeed, we were convinced from the beginning of our work that there were no such things as bare social facts; facts are embedded in theory and social practices. For this reason, we felt compelled to provide and to develop a theory of rape which attempted to explain rape, a theory which did not assume either the framework of a male-supremacist society or the simple view that socialization mechanisms are responsible for the social ills of women.

The main conclusion to be drawn from our work is that rape is a product of a very specific kind of society and of the social relations characteristic of it. Only fundamental changes in that society's legal and social structures will, ultimately, solve the problem of rape. So long as private property exists, there will be institutionalized and structured inquality; so long as women remain forms of private property, there will be institutionalized and structured sexual inequality. It is the unequal legal status of men and women within society that is the fundamental root cause of this and many other problems, and for this reason, changes within those structures must be given priority in a strategy of social change.

The main thrust of our recommendations is directed towards changing the law and changing public attitudes. It is our belief that changes in attitudes alone are not enough; the awareness of women as full persons under the law must be accompanied by the abolition of legislation and judicial practices which view women as property. New legislation and procedural processes must firmly entrench women's full status as equals with men, in and before the law. But legislative change alone is not sufficient either. A massive campaign of public re-education must be undertaken in order to change generally-held attitudes towards the offence, the victim and the offender. Legislative change alone will do little to alleviate the present problems faced by the victim unless these changes are accompanied by changes in the attitudes of all those involved in the criminal justice system, from police officers to crown attorneys and jurypersons. Juries are, after all, persons affected by trial tactics of various kinds, and so long as juries ultimately have final authority over the disposition of a rape case, only public re-education can bring about the reforms that are needed. All changes, at every level, should be directed towards entrenching the view that rape is wrong because it is a form of assault, and that it is always a potential risk to life. It is within this framework, and this framework alone, that the actions of the accused should be scrutinized and judged.

Perhaps we can look forward to a day when all forms of sexual coercion will be prohibited. But it is clear that persuasive/coercive tactics will be inevitable so long as women do not have rights of sexual and reproductive autonomy. Autonomy does not, of course, mean that women should honour every demand for sexual gratification. That version of "sexual liberation" is simply another aspect of the old status and its underlying assumptions; it still sees the right to female sexuality resting with the male, but extends those rights beyond those of an individual owner/husband. To insist that women are "free" sexually when they sleep with everyone is simply to give all men, rather than only some men, legal rights of access to the female sexual property they want. But genuinely free relationships are possible only between equals, between persons who have an independent right over their own sexuality, and may exercise that right without fear of the social or legal consequences.

It is certainly our belief that rape would cease to be a problem if all persons were sexually and reproductively autonomous, both legally and practically speaking. In such circumstances, women would have no special duties of care with respect to their sexuality, and would owe no duties to anyone with respect to its use and disposition. Consequently, men would not have to bargain for female sexuality, at least in the normal course of events. Nor would they be able to interpret a woman's "no" as being based on anything other than her own real desires. Any actions done against her express lack of agreement could then be seen as nothing but a physically coerced interference with her body against her will.

It would be both unreasonable and unrealistic to prohibit all forms of coercive sexual contact while any vestige remains of the old structures and their attendant ideology. So long as men must bargain for sex, it would be unjust to prohibit all coercive strategies. But clearly there must be limits, and those limits must be agreed upon by both men and women. The law must reflect the perspective of free, autonomous women and not solely that of property-owning men. More importantly, changes in the law and in social attitudes must remove the necessity of any forms of coercion. And that means removing all traces of legal and social structures which accord women a status other than that of full legal persons, with complete autonomy over all aspects of their lives. The twin poles of women's liberation are the right to reproductive control and the right to equal access to the productive labour market. An entrenched right to sexual and reproductive autonomy is a fundamental cornerstone of the rights of women and, indeed, of the rights of all.

recommendations

Since fundamental change of the kind we are advocating will occur as an interplay between the law and public attitudes, there is no one domain in which change is most needed. Change must take place at all levels, and in all spheres, simultaneously. If priorities must be set, we certainly believe that changes in legislation, police practices and court procedures, are among the most important. But because such changes cannot be effective unless they are understood and accepted by the general public, they must be accompanied by widespread public education; the public must understand both the objectives which those changes are meant to effect, and the reasons why those specific changes are the best means of achieving the desired objectives. The problem of rape will not disappear until the most basic attitudes towards male and female relationships are changed, but these attitudes will change only if structural changes and public education are carried on in tandem.

The primary legislative change which must be made is the deletion of rape from the "Sexual Offences" section of the Criminal Code. New assault offences should be created to define prohibited behaviour, on the basis of principles which acknowledge the full equality of men and women. The precise principles to be implemented should include the following:

1. The physically coerced use of another person's body for any purpose whatsoever is wrong in itself.
2. The use of a person's body for a sexual purpose, in physically coercive circumstances, is wrong regardless of who that person is, or of the "value" which that person is believed by others to have.
3. Such acts are wrong whether or not any harm was intended, or actually inflicted upon the victim. Sexual attacks, no less than any others, always create a risk of harm; those who commit them are responsible for the creation of such risk and for any harm that occurs. Such risk is a clearly foreseeable consequence of physically coercive behaviour, regardless of what is intended or of what in fact transpires.
4. The use or threat of physical force is sufficient to negate any presumption of consent to the act in question, sexual or otherwise. "Proof" of lack of consent is therefore unnecessary, and medical corroboration of the victim's resistance is therefore irrelevant.
5. It is irrelevant whether the act is perpetrated by a male or a female, on a male or a female.
6. The legal relationship existing between the offender and the victim prior to, at the time of, or following the offence is also irrelevant.

These recommendations must be bolstered by removing from the *Evidence Act* those sections which permit the cross-examination of rape victims on their personal, especially sexual, history. These sections should be replaced by a new section stipulating that such questions are inadmissible. The defence can always introduce evidence that, in a particular case, such questions should be admissible because they are relevant, but the onus should be on the defence to demonstrate relevance before they can be allowed. *The character of the rape victim is not a matter in issue* and this fact must be clearly articulated within the framework of criminal law and criminal procedure.

courtroom procedures

In court, all rape victims must be accorded their full rights of redress under the law. It is the responsibility of crown attorneys to bring even the most "problematic" cases to trial, and to encourage the police to bring all possible rape cases to preliminary hearing. Retarded victims, or victims with a history of mental illness, should not be denied their day in court; nor should victims of low socio-economic status or "dubious reputation" be treated as less credible than other victims.

Crown attorneys should also take on the responsibility of preparing rape victims for trial and preliminary hearing. To this end, and in order to strengthen the prosecution's case, the same crown attorney should act in both phases of the judicial process. In court the crown should energetically represent a rape victim's interests, by objecting to the irrelevant and prejudicial questions of defence lawyers. Similarly, the presiding judge should scrupulously prevent such questions from being asked.

Because many rape victims perceive themselves to be greatly "devalued" by the act (and are perceived by others in the same way), punishment for the crime should suit the degree of damage felt by the victim.

police procedures

While we were most impressed with the active support which the police give to rape victims, we felt that their supportive role could be made more effective in a number of ways. First, it seems apparent that the victim is most comfortable when she does not have to deal with large numbers of police officers. There is no uniform policy governing the investigation of rape cases in Metropolitan Toronto: in some divisions, it is standard practice to interview the victim in the division station, sometimes by different police officers of varying ranks, and on a number of different occasions; in others, the victim is never taken to the station, and is interviewed only by a team of detectives who remain with her throughout the case. From the point of view of both the police and the victim, the latter policy is clearly preferable and should be adopted uniformly. A strong relation of trust and support is much more likely to develop between the victim and the police in such circumstances, and the victim is much less likely to gain the impression that she is being "grilled" by different persons in an attempt to find or generate loopholes in her story. It is of tremendous benefit to have the interview occur in the victim's residence and to postpone detailed questioning about the event until some time following its occurrence.

Since the victim will often first come into contact with a patrolman, all patrolmen should be routinely instructed in the handling of such cases. They should be as supportive with the victim as possible, and should not ask her questions which she will have to relate again to the detectives assigned to her case. It also seems advisable that some detectives be singled out as specialists in the area, and that all rape cases be dealt with by them. However, it seems less clear that the police handling of rape cases should be organized on anything above the divisional level. Close geographical proximity between the victim and the investigating officers is one of the main sources of her support, particularly in those cases where the victim fears reprisals, and in urban areas as large as Metropolitan Toronto, it may be advisable to have decentralized, divisionally identified, teams of specialized investigators. The controlling principle behind any such reorganization of police resources should be to provide the most supportive, easily accessible facilities possible, and continuity of personnel is the single most important feature of such support. It is our belief that the initial contact between victim and police strongly affects her judgment to proceed to trial, and it is thus in the interest of the police to establish the best relations possible from the outset. Organization of the type outlined above will most effectively secure the co-operation of the victim, and will lead to the loss of fewer cases through the complainant's unwillingness to participate.

There is an additional reason for arguing that detectives specializing in rape offences should not be organized above the divisional level. The divisional identity of police officers makes them aware of the particular problems and values shared by the residents in their jurisdiction. They come to know the people that they must deal with, and to understand the roles that are expected of them.

Nor are these roles merely those we most typically associate with a "policing function". As was apparent even in our geographically limited study, there are differences in the ways the public perceives a legitimate police role. In some communities the police are regarded as primary problem solvers, whether or not these problems come clearly within the bounds of the criminal law. Among the genuinely unfounded cases in our study, for example, one woman appeared to want nothing more than a little attention, and two others merely wanted an outlet for their anger at having been abused. These women saw the police as serving their needs; the police were people they could talk to, whom they felt understood their problems. This would not be their feeling if police officers were not seen as members of the community to which these complainants belonged. The closer the ties between police and community, the better police-community relations will be, and the more effective the preventive role police can play in crime control.

If women perceive police officers as men who will be responsive to their complaints, then they will be more likely to report rape offences. Women from every class and social strata are raped, and the greater the extent to which they can identify with the police officers whom they may need to contact, the greater the likelihood that they will report. This is not to say that a woman would not complain to a detective from another area, whom she does not perceive as a member of her community, but she will be more likely to report to someone she does know, and with whom she has a basic relation of trust.

Also, since it cannot be denied that some bias does exist on the part of individual police officers, by virtue of their being particular human beings with specific histories and social backgrounds, it seems reasonable to assume that such biases will be tempered by familiarity with the people who live and work within the area of their jurisdiction. One cannot remain long with any group of people without coming to understand their perspective, even if one falls short of adopting that perspective, or of endorsing the values arising out of it. Police officers familiar with the values and socialization processes affecting the women within the communities they police will be more responsive to their rape complaints than might be the case if those complaints were received by someone outside that social milieu. The processing of rape complaints at the divisional level will ensure that all such complaints will be adequately investigated regardless of the victim's class and social status, and that all women, regardless of such socio-economic factors, will feel more comfortable about reporting.

The danger of a centralized rape squad is that it may become a prisoner of its own biases and favour some kinds of complainants over others. This is a very real danger so long as the police are forced to filter forward only those cases with the best chance of successful outcome at trial. As things now stand, the best cases involve only certain kinds of victims: young, middle-class women who are highly emotional, who are either virgins living at home and going to school, or chastely within the bonds of monogamous marriage, who do not drink in public, have no history of mental illness, are not known for frequenting public places where they establish contact with male strangers, who do not hitch-hike, accept rides from strangers, or willingly accompany men to their residences. It would be virtually impossible for a centralized rape squad not to favour such women and not to filter out cases involving complainants who do not conform to this picture. No matter how understandable the motives behind this selective process, it cannot be allowed to deny justice to the many women who have legitimate complaints but do not get their day in court because they fail to exhibit these features.

All women, regardless of age, class, marital status, or other factors, deserve the protection and redress of the law. But at the present time, many women are unfairly treated because they have less "credibility" than other women, or because their cases present problems which some others do not. It is, thus, of the utmost importance that no woman fail to report because she feels uncomfortable about reporting to someone outside her own peer group, and no woman should be accorded less credibility than others because she has to report outside her own peer group. For these reasons, we believe that a centralized rape squad should not be established in Metropolitan Toronto, or in any other large centre in Canada which displays the variety of class and social structure typical of such urban conglomerations. Equal protection demands equality of access and equality of treatment. We believe that this can best be accomplished by introducing specialized investigative teams of detectives at the divisional level only.

And we believe that the best way to secure equal treatment of all victims reporting rape is to give all police officers specialized training. All potential police officers should be made aware of the history and evolution of rape as an offence, and of the problems surrounding the handling of rape cases. Such "sensitivity" training would do more to reduce the present difficulties of individual rape complainants than anything else. The same kind of training should also be routinely offered to crown attorneys and other officers of the court. Clearly the present practice of filtering rape cases out of the judicial system on the basis of judgments made about the complainant's value must be stopped, but it cannot be stopped until all those who are a part of the process come to understand that rape is an offence which can be committed against any kind of woman, regardless of any other facts about her.

the young victim

As we pointed out in chapter 5, the parents of very young rape victims sometimes seek the aid of the police in censuring behaviour which they regard as "promiscuous". We would recommend that, wherever such a situation seems a distinct possibility, the case be turned over to the Youth Bureau or to someone better able to deal with the problem as one of interpersonal, familial conflict. The victim should not be made to feel that her sexual conduct is being disapproved of, and punished, by the legal system. She hardly needs to be told that bringing a false charge is wrong; she knows that it is, but she is often left very little option in order to avoid punitive treatment from her parents, or others in authority over her. Her knowledge that what she is doing is wrong, and that she doesn't want to do it, is in fact what leads to her hostility, and everything possible should be done by the police to ensure the minimization of such internal conflicts. A woman who finds herself in this position—who is forced to tell lies to protect herself from overly judgmental and punitive parents—is likely to end up with little respect for the judgments of her parents or for those which she believes are being expressed by the legal system through the police. Such an outcome is clearly undesirable from the point of view of both the woman and the police.

Police officers should be made as sensitive as possible to this sort of problem and should not allow themselves to be swayed by parents who portray their daughters as habitually "promiscuous". They should reprimand parents who push for charges against the wishes of the victim, and should investigate each case as fully as possible despite parental disbelief. Wherever possible, the complainant should be interviewed in the absence of her parents, particularly when they rather than she have reported the offence, and as strongly supportive a milieu as possible should be established in order to protect her from possible punishment. Parents who are eager to pursue charges against the wishes of the victim ought to be counselled, as should those who refuse to acknowledge the commission of an offence despite good evidence to the contrary. It is they, and not the complainant, who are creating the problem. No complainant should be dismissed because of parental disbelief, and no complainant should be humiliated because of parental puritanism.

the role of rape crisis centres

Until such time as the changes which we have recommended begin to take place, we believe that rape crisis centres have an important role to play and that they deserve special mention within this context. One of the most significant developments around the whole issue of rape has been the establishment of rape crisis centres. At the moment, there are approximately 22 such centres in Canada. In addition to providing a much-needed service to victims, rape crisis centres have focused public attention on rape and have pinpointed specific areas of difficulty and injustice. In the long run, it is almost certain that their most lasting contribution will be their educative function. While they were born of the need to provide supportive services to rape victims, changes of the kind we are recommending will mean that these services will one day no longer be required. They should not be required now, but they are, and will continue to be needed for some time.

The functions of rape crisis centres are essentially three-fold. First, they provide a supportive, non-judgmental milieu for the victim, and assist her in dealing with the many problems she will face, whether or not she reports the offence and becomes involved in the criminal justice system. They provide facilities where rape victims can talk to one another and come to appreciate that they are not rare cases, but that they share feelings of isolation, despair, helplessness and anger, feelings which are a product of those public attitudes which persist in seeing rape as a "sexual" offence to be kept out of the public eye and mind, surrounded by a conspiracy of silence. This is essentially a health service, and its necessity and benefit should be clearly recognized and supported, financially and otherwise.

Secondly, crisis centres perform a para-legal function by counselling rape victims about what they can expect from the judicial system if they report the offence, and by accompanying victims who do wish to report through all the phases of the judicial process in which they may become involved. Again, while there should not be any need for such personnel, their fulfillment of this need should be socially recognized and supported. Rape crisis centres should have the same status as those "store-front" legal operations designed to provide legal counsel for people who would not otherwise get it. Rape victims desperately require this kind of assistance because no one else currently supplies it; their purely theoretical belief is that the Crown will take care of things. But until the Crown does take a more active interest in the needs of rape victims for support and counselling, there is a very definite need for the services which rape crisis centres now provide.

Allied with these para-legal services is one further function which we believe to be among the most effective strategies for change. Nothing quite brings home the problem which rape presents to the victim like sitting through a rape trial. And nothing makes clearer to the officers of the Court how objectionable much of their behaviour is, than having it monitored by others who are critical of the attitudes and conduct they display. Rape crisis workers can play a very effective role in promoting change at the judicial level, simply by being present in the courtroom and by confronting officers of the Court with their own attitudes and behaviour. We are not suggesting disruptive courtroom behaviour. In fact we would be among the first to caution against any such behaviour, since it is almost certain to make things more uncomfortable for the victim and to ensure an unsatisfactory trial outcome. The first consideration is always the particular victim on the stand, and nothing should be done to make the trial more of an ordeal than it already is. But simply being there, finding out who the officers of the Court are, and talking with them over coffee, can do a great deal to make them change their attitudes and begin acting in ways which are consistent with a fair and unbiased assessment of the issues.

The third main function of rape crisis centres is that of public education. Because they are now among the most knowledgeable people about rape and its problems, rape crisis centre volunteers are in an ideal position to engage in large and small-scale public education. Most major Canadian cities have given widespread media coverage to rape crisis centres and this has been absolutely invaluable. But in addition to mass media education, there are numerous other educative tasks rape crisis workers can and do perform, from talking to small groups of high-school students, to organizing workshops for medical, police, and court officials. At the moment, apart from the media coverage which was, at least in the beginning, motivated as much by the desire to exploit potentially "sensational" news as it was to promote a better understanding of rape, many of these efforts are hindered by the fact that the public still does not want to hear about the problem. Attempts to talk with high-school women have consistently met with resistance from school and school-board authorities, who persist in the belief that rape really doesn't happen all that often, that when it does it probably isn't all the fault of the offender, and that it is dangerous to talk about it because it may generate a "panic". These attitudes are indefensible in light of the facts, and school officials should do all that they can to promote public discussion of the issues among both male and female students. Since so many of the problems surrounding rape concern attitudes, educational authorities should recognize, promote and support such public discussions, and rape crisis centres should be funded to perform this essential service.

A comparatively minor, but nonetheless important and distinguishable function that rape crisis centres have is that of research. Since they are, at the moment, the only source of data on unreported rape, they can perform a major service in keeping records of the cases dealt with, noting the numbers and reasons for reporting and non-reporting. Since they establish close and intimate contact with the victims, they are often in an ideal position to carry out sensitive interviews designed to elicit the victim's deep feelings about how she has been affected by the rape and subsequent events. However, we believe that this research should be co-ordinated, and that it should be conducted within a framework which sees the victim, and her confidential relations with rape crisis volunteers, as absolutely primary and inviolable. Rape crisis centre workers frequently find themselves being asked for information which they cannot in conscience provide, and it is therefore unrealistic to expect them to fulfill a research function which is in conflict with their primary obligation to the victim. We are in complete agreement with the decision to establish a national organization of rape crisis centres which will have as one of its major functions the co-ordination of such research and the limitation of this function so that it in no way conflicts with the primary objectives such organizations have.

But the whole question of research, and its relation to the supportive function rape crisis centres play, is only one aspect of the whole problem of possible conflicts of interest in this area. If rape crisis centres are to be able to play the supportive, para-legal, and educational roles they do, they must be able to do so *independent* of the other parts of the social, medical, legal and educational processes with which they will come in contact. Above all, rape crisis centres must be able to act independently of the control of any of the other processes which affect the victims. While they must, to perform a useful supportive service to victims, have good relations with the local police agency, they cannot work *with* the police without jeopardizing their ability to reach rape victims who do not wish to report. Similarly, they cannot function as victim-oriented, para-legals if they are working in close conjunction with officers of the Court. Above all, rape crisis centres must not come to be seen as part of the establishment processes with which rape victims currently come in contact. If they do, they will become part of the problem rather than part of the solution. They must continue to remain outside the institutionalized framework that deals with the problem. They cannot perform a supportive service for all rape victims, or a critical para-legal and educational function, if they are in any way controlled by those institutional structures. Thus, rape crisis centres must be funded in such a way that control does not, and cannot, pass from their hands into the hands of those who have a vested interest either in seeing rape cases dealt with in one way rather than another, or in protecting themselves from criticism. It is not an easy role to play, but it is at the moment an essential role; rape crisis centres cannot function as impartial "ombudsmen" if their funding is dependent on the institutions they may have to criticize. Thus, we believe that funding for rape crisis centres should come from a federal body, clearly ear-marked for the control of individual rape crisis centres, for purposes which are, and must remain, outside the in-stitutionalized structures. It must not be administered through those parts of the process that are themselves affected, and must not depend on working in conjunction with those institutions.

further research objectives

Despite what we now know about rape in Canada, there is still a very great deal that we do not know. The first, and major, research objec-tive for the future should be to elicit a truly national picture of the offence and its incidence, of differences in reporting rates and report-ing populations, differences in police handling of cases, differences in judicial procedures, and differences in rates of conviction. We now know that these differences are significant from one province to another, and within specific locales in individual provinces. Upon the completion of a large study in British Columbia, designed to elicit data comparable with the work already completed in Ontario, we will have a somewhat better picture of the urban phenomenon of rape, and of similarities and differences in court processing between at least two provinces.[1] But we need more studies of this type if we are to uncover both regional differences and regional similarities. We also need a thorough study of rape in rural and sub-rural communities. We would hope that within the next five years, major studies reflecting the re-gional make-up of Canadian society will have been completed in at least four, major, Canadian urban centres, and at least one good study of a rural area under R.C.M.P. jurisdiction will have been completed. Not until such comparative data is available will we be able to claim any knowledge of the national picture which rape presents.

One of the major reasons for eliciting information of this type is that without it, we have no basis for advocating changes in purely local administration of justice. Until we understand not only the similarities, but also the differences, we cannot begin to pinpoint specific variables which account for differences in reporting rates, reporting populations, rates of apprehension, and conviction. To know what can work, we need to know what does and does not work.

Another, somewhat minor but nonetheless important research task is to record the research already done, in progress, or planned for the future. As interest in rape reflects a number of different perspectives—those of the institutions affected, rape victims, rape crisis centres, correctional services, as well as independent researchers—it is important to recover information which is available but little known, and to know what is being done in all of these various areas. A small project to begin this task has just been completed,[2] and it is our hope that this will lead to the formation of a central registry of research functions and objectives.

Again, there is a substantive rather than a purely fact-gathering reason for such studies. Since so much of the present interest in rape is focused on the effects of rape and subsequent events on the victim, there is quite naturally a strong desire to establish contact with rape victims and to interview them. But in doing this, the researcher, no matter what his or her perspective, becomes a part of the process the rape victim encounters. Research becomes yet another phase of the protracted process in which the victim, whether reporting or nonreporting, becomes enmeshed. This in itself is cause for concern, but it is cause for even greater concern insofar as it can come to affect the victim either beneficially or adversely. It would be a sad irony to discover that the very research designed to help solve the problem in fact exacerbates it for individual victims. This is not a matter to be taken lightly, and any projected research dealing with rape victims must ensure that the risk of further trauma to the victim is absolutely minimal. While researchers normally perceive themselves as "objective" investigators, who are unconcerned with what happens as a consequence of the *doing* of the research, we believe that this is not a defensible perspective so far as rape is concerned. Research must be undertaken for the purpose of assisting the victim, of using research as a vehicle for her benefit even if that means jeopardizing the objectivity of the research itself. The researcher becomes a person who has a potential effect on the victim, and the moral responsibility that imposes cannot be denied on the superficial ground of the need for "objectivity". It is essential to know what type of research is projected, so that guidelines may be provided for its conduct.

But there is, of course, one glaring omission from all that we have said so far. What about the offender? He, after all, is the immediate cause of the problem. It is entirely purposeless to elicit all the information that we have suggested needs gathering, and to propose changes which will make it less traumatic for the victim to report a rape occurrence, and easier to gain conviction of rape offenders, if we know nothing about the offender himself. What strategies can be adopted either to "rehabilitate" him or to deter him from committing future offences? The little we know now suggests that nothing we are currently doing does anything at all for the offender. As we noted earlier, McCaldon concludes gloomily that rape offenders do not have a high therapeutic potential.[3] This is hardly surprising, however, given the theory which we believe explains rape. If the convicted rapist is in no sense "abnormal", from the perspective of a society in which coercive sexuality is the norm and in which women are regarded as sexual property, then nothing short of total re-education is going to affect his beliefs and the actions which arise out of them. The only function imprisonment can serve is to keep him off the streets for the duration of his sentence. Clearly, we cannot hope to cure the individual convicted rapist while society and social attitudes remain unchanged. Rape will only disappear once fundamental social changes are effected. Nevertheless, because he is a potential risk to society, something must be done to ensure that the risk he creates is minimized.

It is our belief that research on the offender is badly needed, and that this research should take the form of attitudinal studies designed to elicit the framework in which he understands his own sexuality, that of other men, and that of women. Not until we understand that framework, from his perspective, can we possibly design strategies for changing that framework, thus making it unnecessary for him to commit the offences he does. Further, since prison does nothing to affect the rapist's long-range pattern of behaviour, some research is needed into the possibilities of other forms of social control. Perhaps long-term supervised participation in group therapy sessions is more of a real answer to the problem than simple confinement. But what this entails, of course, is changing our attitudes to both the misogyny characteristic of the rapist and other males, and to the acceptability of coercive sexuality. If we can come to see misogyny as abnormal then perhaps we can actually do something useful for the offender and for the other members of society to whom he is a menace. It is our belief that much behaviour which is considered "normal" for males within this society, should be regarded as "abnormal", and that treatment programmes incorporating these beliefs ought to be devised for dealing with rapists. From the perspective of a sexually egalitarian society, the rapist is abnormal, as of course are many other men who are not labelled rapists. But we have to begin somewhere, and we may as well begin with those who have clearly demonstrated their inability to conform even to the minimal standards of acceptable sexual conduct.[4]

It is our sincere hope that new research objectives will be formulated, with the goal of understanding the warped attitudes toward male and female sexuality which underlie the actions of convicted rapists, and of those who might well be convicted but for the happy presence of better socio-economic circumstances. New concepts of mental abnormality must be developed to cope with this problem, not only to understand it, but to cure it. What may begin as a rehabilitation programme for convicted rapists may well end up providing us with a general, educational blueprint for a non-sexist, sexually egalitarian society; surely means designed to treat the worst cases might be even more effective for the best ones. But it is not until we are prepared to recognize that the misogyny characteristic of the rapist and many other men in society is abnormal—a diagnosable, treatable, illness —that we can even hope to design rehabilitative or other coercive strategies to cure such behavior.

But with this comment, we come to a consideration of the most fundamental of all the changes which must occur if rape is to be ameliorated and, ultimately, eliminated. Nothing short of a complete re-education of all members of society, supported by the resources of all our existing institutions, can possibly bring about our ultimate objective. Not until everyone accepts and cannot escape the reality of the principle that women are socially, legally, economically, and sexually the equals of men, will rape cease to be a problem. It is a big job. We only hope that this book goes some little way toward moving us forward to that sexually egalitarian society all women desire and all men must learn to accept.

appendix a
general occurrence report

METROPOLITAN TORONTO POLICE
GENERAL OCCURRENCE REPORT

(MTP 206)

REV. (7/69)

INSTRUCTIONS: This Report must be HAND-PRINTED, except signature, in BLACK INK, with a ballpoint pen, pressing firmly at all times. When it is necessary to use the reverse side, detach carbon paper and insert other rearranging copies so that the back of the original copy is also the original copy. DESCRIPTIONS of persons and property to be as complete as possible.

appendix b
research instrument *

1. Offence: attempted rape ___ rape ___ indecent assault ___ other ___
2. Date of Research: day ___ month ___ year ___
3. Place of offence: victim's residence ___ offender's residence ___
   vehicle ___ public building ___ public street ___ public park ___
   another residence _____
   details _____
4. Patrol area _____
5. Victim information:
      (a) sex: M ___ F ___
      (b) age ___
      (d) occupation _____
      (e) marital status: (circle)
            M   S   D   Sep   Other
      (f) condition of victim _____
      (c) national origin: (circle)
            Canadian
            American
            Greek
            Italian
            British
            Portuguese
            Chinese
            West Indian
            Other
6. Reported by: (circle)
            father   mother
            victim   friend   boyfriend   husband
            neighbour   other
7. How attacked _____
8. Means of attack (weapons etc.) _____
9. Object of attack (motive, property stolen) _____
10. Vehicle, year & make _____
11. Can suspect(s) be identified?   yes ___   no ___
12. Complainant advised to take out warrant ___ or summons ___
13. Warrant issued: yes ___ no ___
14. Property: all recovered ___ some recovered ___
                none recovered ___ none lost ___ value of property ___
15. Founded ___ Unfounded ___
16. Arrested offender: yes ___ no ___
       (if yes) age ___ nationality _____

   * *This is a facsimile of the form that we used; it contains all the questions asked, but does not necessarily indicate the space allotted to each answer.*

17. Culprit known, action taken ___ comments _____
    Culprit known, no action taken ___ comments _____
    Culprit unknown ___ comments _____
18. Time of: (a) complaint   date _____ time _____
             (b) investigation
             (c) report
19. How complaint received: personal at station ___ phone ___
                            at scene ___
                            other _____
20. Description of offender(s) by victim: age, height, weight, build, complexion, hair, clothing, peculiarities, etc. _____
21. Description of victim _____
22. Situation, general description _____
23. Supplementary report(s). (Note dates and number of report; add sheet if necessary.) _____
24. Evidence retained by police _____
25. Offender's record of arrest (supplementary): _____
    (a) age _____
    (b) date of birth _____
    (c) sex: M   F
    (d) colour _____
    (e) occupation _____
    (f) place of birth _____
26. Date and time of arrest _____
27. Location of arrest _____
28. Apparent injuries _____
29. Previous arrests _____

notes

chapter 1

1. Susan Griffin, "Rape: The All-American Crime", pp. 26-35.
2. Susan Brownmiller, *Against Our Will*.
3. J.W. Mohr, "Rape and Attempted Rape".
4. Debra J. Lewis, "Rape in Toronto".

chapter 2

1. Lorenne M.G. Clark, Margaret Barr-Carley and Mary Ward, "A Study of Rape in Canada: Phases A and B". This work was funded by the National Law Reform Commission and consisted of an analysis of all rape cases going at least to preliminary hearing in the Judicial District of York (Metropolitan Toronto), Province of Ontario, 1970-73, and in-depth interviewing of rape victims whose cases went at least to preliminary hearing in this jurisdiction during this time period. Ms. Barr-Carley and Ms. Ward were employed as research assistants on these phases of the research and also utilized the data collected as the bases of M.A. theses in criminology: Margaret Barr-Carley, "An Examination of Rape Cases Going to Preliminary Hearing, 1970-73; Mary Ward, "Rape: A Descriptive Study Involving In-Depth Interviews with Victims whose Cases Proceeded to Preliminary Hearing, 1970-73".

Lorenne M.G. Clark and Simon Armstrong, "A Review of Past, Present and Projected Rape Research". This report includes a complete bibliography of rape research in Canada, which is a revision of an earlier rape bibliography compiled by Chappell, Geis and Fogarty in the United States as part of a major American study of rape.

Lorenne M.G. Clark and Debra J. Lewis, "A Study of Rape in Canada: Phases C and D". This research was funded by the Donner Foundation and exactly parallels the research completed in Ontario.

2. *Martin's Annual Criminal Code, 1972*, pp. 97-98.

3. Ibid., p. 99.

4. Ibid., p. 97.

5. Ibid., p. 91.

6. Menachem Amir, *Patterns in Forcible Rape*. This was a study of 646 reported rapes in Philadelphia during 1958 and 1960.

7. Duncan Chappell and Susan Singer, "Rape in New York City". This was a study of 704 reports of rape or attempted rape in New York City between 1 February, 1970 and 31 January, 1972.

8. Duncan Chappell, Gilbert Geis, Stephen Schafer and Larry Siegel, "Forcible Rape in Boston and Los Angeles". This was a study of 136 cases of rape reported in Los Angeles and 46 reported rapes in Boston, during 1967.

9. J.W. Mohr, "Rape and Attempted Rape". This was a study of 26 "founded" rape reports leading to a charge in Metropolitan Toronto between 1 November, 1961 and 31 October, 1962.

10. C.A.D. Ringrose, "Sociological, Medical and Legal Aspects of Rape". This was a study of 255 cases of rape reported to the Edmonton Police Department. This publication does not give the dates covered by the study, but says that it took place within "a recent three year period".

11. R.J. McCaldon, "Rape". This was a study of 30 convicted rapists serving their sentences in Kingston Penitentiary.

12. Chappell and Singer, "Rape in New York City", p.8.

13. Roger Hood and Richard Sparks, *Key Issues in Criminology*, p. 32.

14. At the First National Conference of Canadian Rape Crisis Centres, held in Ottawa, 20-22 June, 1975, a national body was formed to outline research objectives and ensure competent research into rape.

15. It is often argued that very few rapes lead to murder, and that there is a qualitative difference between rapists, and those offenders who commit "blood-lust" murders. (See, for example, B. Karpman's *Sexual Offender and His Offenses*.) However, this hypothesis has not, in our view, been substantiated. This question will be discussed more fully in chapters 9 and 11.

chapter 3

1. The Metropolitan Toronto Police Department is organized into a number of divisions, and the case will be dealt with in the division where the offence occurred.

2. Police practices may vary even within one jurisdiction; in Metropolitan Toronto, for example, there is no uniform procedure. Some divisions routinely interview rape complainants at the division station. Others assign detectives to the case immediately and interview the victim at her residence. Some divisions vary their practice according to such contingent factors as the resources available to them, or the time of the report. Some recommendations for the organization of police resources will be discussed at the end of this book.

3. Lorenne M.G. Clark, Margaret Barr-Carley and Mary Ward, "A Study of Rape in Canada: Phases A and B", pp. 70-72. One rape victim interviewed for this study had been asked to identify her assailant from among a crowd of people in a bus depot. She did so without difficulty.

4. Ibid. Bail was granted in 63.6% of the rape cases proceeding to trial in Metropolitan Toronto in 1970-74, and denied in 5.4%. No information regarding bail was available in the remaining 31.0% of cases.

5. *Criminal Law Review, 1959*, p. 450.

6. J. de N. Kennedy, O.B.E., Q.C., *Aids to Jury Charges (Criminal)*, 2d ed. (Agincourt, Ontario: Canada Law Book Limited, 1975), p. 205.

7. *133 Canadian Criminal Cases*, 1962, p. 103.

8. We are not proposing that such evidence be allowed in a rape trial. It would prejudice the jury against the defendant and undermine his civil rights. However, if prejudicial information of this sort cannot be used against the defendant, similar prejudicial information should not be used against the victim, and for the same reasons.

9. *Martin's Annual Criminal Code 1975: First Supplement* (Agincourt: Canada Law Book Limited, 1975), p. 1.

10. Ibid., p.6.

11. This has already been demonstrated, in at least one court judgment made since the new amendments to the Criminal Code became law. In the case of *Regina v. Klaus Paul* (November 15, 1976, Ontario Supreme Court), it was held that the common law of England continues to apply per section 7(2) of the Criminal Code, and corroboration remains desirable, though not mandatory. *Weekly Criminal Bulletin*, no. 9 (December, 1976), p. 10.

12. *Crankshaw's Criminal Code of Canada*, 7th ed., 1959, p. 863.

13. J. de N. Kennedy, *Aids to Jury Charges*, p. 204.

14. Clark, Barr-Carley and Ward, "Rape in Canada: Phases A and B", pp. 37-46.

15. Since 1976 the grand jury has been abolished in Ontario.

16. Under the "Sexual Offences" section of the Canadian Criminal Code, rape is defined as a major offence. This section also includes lesser, or minor offences such as "indecent assault, female" and "attempted rape". When a person is charged with the major offence of rape, he may also be charged with lesser, included offences—that is, offences which are constituted by some, but not all, of the same elements as the major offence.

For example, an act of sexual contact is rape if and only if some penetration of the vagina by the penis has taken place. If penetration was attempted, but cannot be proven to have taken place, then the accused can be charged with either or both of "attempted rape" and "indecent assault, female", since the behaviour which defines them as offences is also part of the behaviour that defines rape. The difference is that rape includes more elements. Thus, an offender may decide that he will get a shorter sentence by pleading guilty to a lesser offence. At trial, if penetration cannot be proved, the charge against the defendant may be reduced to the lesser offence. If the jury does not believe that the accused should be convicted of rape but believes that he did do something illegal, they may acquit him of rape but find him guilty of a lesser offence.

17. Clark, Barr-Carley and Ward, "Rape in Canada: Phases A and B", p. 121. This study found that 4.7% of cases terminated following the grand jury, with the return of a "no" bill.

18. Ibid., pp. 42-44.

19. *Crime Statistics, 1971*, pp. 35-46.

20. Twenty-five of the 42 F cases in our study were cleared by arrest. See chapter 3, note 30 for further details.

21. *Crime Statistics, 1971*, p. 38. The number of persons actually charged with rape in Canada in 1971 is difficult to ascertain. Of the 1230 cases reported by Statistics Canada (p. 21), 547 cases are listed as having been "cleared by charge". However, the provincial breakdowns provided on pp. 35-46 seem to indicate that *600 persons* were charged. The difference may indicate that some of the 547 cases involved multiple offenders. However, on p. 21 it is stated that 718 persons were charged, leaving a difference of 118 persons who are not listed on pp. 35-46. This is confusing enough, but on p. 38, the figure given for the number of persons charged with rape in Canada is 119. This figure excludes those charged with rape in Alberta and Quebec. (No reasons for this exclusion are given.) Adding the totals for those two provinces as given in the provincial breakdowns, 103 and 28 respectively, yields neither the figure 600 nor the figure 718. Perhaps the explanation is that only 119 persons charged with rape, outside of Alberta and Quebec, actually went to trial on that charge. If so, it would be useful to know what happened to the remaining cases. Between charge and trial, some 468 or 350 charges simply disappear.

22. *Crime Statistics 1971*, p. 38. Of course, if one calculates the conviction rate on the basis of 718 or 600 persons charged, the conviction rate is considerably lower—9.0% and 10.8% respectively.

23. *Statistics of Criminal and Other Offences* (Dominion Bureau of Statistics, 1962), p. 40.

24. J.W. Mohr, "Rape and Attempted Rape", p. 28.

25. B. Glueck, "Persons Convicted of Crimes Involving Sexual Aberrations", p. 2.

27. Ibid. This study found that 32.1% of defendants who were charged and went to trial in the Province of Ontario, Judicial District of York, 1970-73, were convicted of rape, and a further 19.1% were acquitted of rape but found guilty of a lesser offence. Thus, of those charged with rape, 51.2% were found guilty of rape or a lesser offence.

28. *Crime Statistics*, 1971, p. 12.

29. *Martin's Annual Criminal Code, 1972*, pp. 97-98.

30. Sentences in excess of eight years indicate either a very brutal rape or a case in which the offender has a past or present history of diagnosable mental abnormality. Sentences from ten years and up usually mean that the offender goes to an institution for the criminally insane. Occasionally such persons become eligible for sentence under preventive detention as "Dangerous Sexual Offenders", in accordance with the provisions under section 689 of the Canadian Criminal Code (*Martin's Annual Criminal Code, 1972*, p. 534). This legislation is more widely used in some jurisdictions than in others, but is almost always reserved for an accused who has been diagnosed as severely abnormal, and has a long history of psychiatric treatment.

31. *Crime Statistics, 1971*, p. 38 and p. 78.

32. Clark, Barr-Carley and Ward, "Rape in Canada: Phases A and B", p. 122.

33. *Crime Statistics, 1971*, p. 38 and p. 78.

34. However, only 25 of the 42 founded cases were thereby cleared by arrest since two cases involved multiple offenders. One was a pair-rape, and the other was a group rape involving 6 offenders. Thus, the clearance rate, by *case*, is 59.5%. But this resulted in the arrest of 32, or 66.6% of the total of 48 offenders involved in the founded cases.

chapter 4

1. *Crime Statistics, 1961*, p. 49.

2. *Crime Statistics, 1971*, p. 21.

3. The Metropolitan Toronto Police Department prepared a tabulated sheet showing the number of rapes reported to them over this five-year period, and calculated the percentage increase on the basis of these figures.

4. Roger Hood and Richard Sparks, *Key Issues in Criminology*, p. 32.

5. Andra Medea and Kathleen Thompson, *Against Rape*, p. 135. The authors outline their research method as follows: "Questionnaires on rape were published in several underground papers and distributed at various rape conferences."(p. 133) They were well aware of the bias in the sample that they obtained this way, but their results are nonetheless valuable as it is almost impossible to obtain a widely representative sample of rape occurrences. Certainly, their bias is no worse than if they had looked only at rape cases reported to the police.

6. The Metropolitan Toronto Police Department thought that the 40% reporting rate was most probable, but did not think the 10% rate was all that unlikely. The 10% rate has been quoted by crown attorneys and others

involved in the judicial process, and was the rate quoted by an R.C.M.P. officer serving in a non-urban jurisdiction.

7. We found that 42% of the rape cases in our study occurred between midnight and 6:00 a.m., and that a further 36% occurred between 6:00 p.m. and midnight.

FORCIBLE RAPE COMPLAINTS
IN TORONTO
BY TIME OF OCCURRENCE

Time	No. of Cases	Percentage
2400–0559	42	42.0
0600–1159	9	9.0
1200–1759	13	13.0
1800–2359	36	36.0
Total	*100*	*100.0*

NOTE: No information was available in 4 cases.

8. We found that the peak season occurred in the late summer months. The pattern was less distinct for founded reports only, but peaks were still apparent, falling in September and October.

MONTHLY COMPARISON OF
FORCIBLE RAPE COMPLAINTS
IN TORONTO AND NEW YORK CITY

	Toronto *		*New York City* **	
Month	*No. of Cases*	*Percentage*	*No. of Cases*	*Percentage*
January	9	8.7	32	8.2
February	5	4.8	24	6.2
March	3	2.9	31	8.0
April	8	7.7	32	8.2
May	5	4.8	31	8.0
June	9	8.7	35	9.0
July	12	11.5	36	9.3
August	13	12.5	33	8.5
September	14	13.5	33	8.5
October	9	8.7	33	8.5
November	9	8.7	32	8.2
December	8	7.7	37	9.5
Total	*104*	*100.2*	*389*	*100.1*

* Clark/Lewis Study, reports made in 1970.
** Chappell and Singer, p. 56, reports made 1970–1972.

Long-term, seasonally-adjusted rates for the U.S. show a well-established pattern, with the majority of rapes occurring from May to September. On the other hand, no such seasonal pattern emerged in the New York City or Los Angeles data: Duncan Chappell and Susan Singer, "Rape in New York City", p. 8 and p. 10; Menachem Amir, *Patterns in Forcible Rape*, p. 80; Duncan Chappell, Gilbert Geis, Stephen Schafer and Larry Siegel, "Forcible Rape in Boston and Los Angeles", p. 185.

While little research of this kind has been done in Canada, our findings are thoroughly consistent with the results of the other two Canadian studies: J. W. Mohr, "Rape and Attempted Rape", pp. 12–13; C.A.D. Ringrose, "Sociological, Medical and Legal Aspects of Rape", p. 10.

9.   FORCIBLE RAPE COMPLAINTS IN TORONTO
                        BY DAY OF WEEK

Day	No. of Cases	Percentage
Monday	11	10.9
Tuesday	16	15.8
Wednesday	17	16.8
Thursday	13	12.9
Friday	20	19.8
Saturday	7	6.9
Sunday	17	16.8
Total	101	99.9

NOTE: No information was available in 3 cases.

In Los Angeles and Philadelphia, 54% and 42.5% respectively of rapes occurred on Saturday and Sunday. This trend was less marked in New York City, where 34.5% of rapes occurred on weekends. (Duncan Chappell and Susan Singer, "Rape in New York City", p. 10.) We found no such trend in Toronto, although eight years previously Mohr had found "...the expectation that the weekends would be more heavily loaded than other days is borne out, with the exception of an additional high on Tuesday" (J.W. Mohr, "Rape and Attempted Rape", p. 13).

10.   See, for example, Menachem Amir, *Patterns in Forcible Rape*, p. 148.
11.   R.J. McCaldon, "Rape", p. 41.
12.   J.W. Mohr, "Rape and Attempted Rape", p. 16.
13.   McCaldon, "Rape", p. 40.
14.   All of the cases involving anal intercourse were classified as founded, and Clark, Barr-Carley and Ward report that 17.6% of the cases in their study which proceeded to preliminary hearing involved anal intercourse ("Rape in Canada: Phases A and B", p. 222).

15. Amir, *Patterns in Forcible Rape*, p. 159.
16. Duncan Chappell and Susan Singer, "Rape in New York City", pp. 16-17.
17. Amir, *Patterns in Forcible Rape*, pp. 233-234.
18. Clark, Barr-Carley and Ward, "Rape in Canada: Phases A and B".
19. McCaldon, "Rape", p. 42.
20. This was also the case in New York City (Duncan Chappell and Susan Singer, "Rape in New York City", p. 65); and also in R.J. McCaldon's study ("Rape", p. 42) where only 4% of the offences were committed by "friends" and 10% by "acquaintances".
21. Medea and Thompson, *Against Rape*, p. 142.

chapter 5

1. John M. MacDonald, *Rape Offenders and Their Victims*, p. 76.
2. Menachem Amir, *Patterns in Forcible Rape*, p. 52.
3. R.J. McCaldon, "Rape", p. 42.
4. J.W. Mohr, "Rape and Attempted Rape", p. 6.
5. Lorenne M.G. Clark, Margaret Barr-Carley and Mary Ward, "Rape in Canada: Phases A and B", p. 199.
6. Mohr, "Rape and Attempted Rape", p. 8.
7. McCaldon, "Rape", p. 42.
8. Clark, Barr-Carley and Ward, "Rape in Canada: Phases A and B", p. 201.
9. Ibid., pp. 115-117.
10. Why, for example, could this case not have been prosecuted under Section 148:

> Every male person who, under circumstances that do not amount to rape, has sexual intercourse with a female person
> (a) who is not his wife, and
> (b) who is and who he knows or has good reason to believe is feeble-minded, insane, or is an idiot or imbecile is guilty of an indictable offence and is liable to imprisonment for five years.

11. For a discussion of the "glass-jaw principle", see p. 69 of chapter 11.
12. Police notes on this case were quoted on pp. 35-36 of chapter 2.
13. Mohr, "Rape and Attempted Rape", pp. 30-39.

chapter 6

1. Two other Canadian studies reported similar findings. R.J. McCaldon ("Rape", p. 43) found that 83% of offenders were Caucasian, 10% Canadian Indian, 7% Negro and 0% Oriental. J.W. Mohr ("Rape and Attempted Rape", p. 10) found that 83% of the offenders in his study were Canadian: "All offenders were white, with the exception of one Canadian Negro and one Canadian Indian."

2. R.J. McCaldon, "Rape", p. 43; C.A.D. Ringrose, "Sociological, Medical and Legal Aspects of Rape", p. 1.
3. They were somewhat older than their counterparts in New York City, where just over 25% of the offenders studied were more than thirty years of age, and over 50% were younger than twenty-five. They were also considerably older than the rapists in Mohr's study: only 15.7% of these offenders were over thirty, and only 26.3% were between twenty-five and twenty-nine. Duncan Chappell and Susan Singer, "Rape in New York City", p. 74; J.W. Mohr, "Rape and Attempted Rape", p. 6.
4. Mohr, "Rape and Attempted Rape", p. 7.
5. Ibid., p. 9 and p. 27.
6. McCaldon, "Rape", p. 45.
7. Ibid.
8. See, for example, the following: John M. MacDonald, *Rape Offenders and Their Victims*, p. 55; U.S. Presidential Commission on Law Enforcement and the Administration of Justice, 1967; K. Svalastoga, "Rape and Social Structure", p. 48.
9. However, this aspect of rape has recently been discussed by Diana Russell in *The Politics of Rape*. See especially chapters 11-16 and 23.
10. MacDonald, *Rape Offenders and Their Victims*, p. 66.
11. Ibid., p. 70.
12. Ibid., p. 71.
13. Ibid.
14. McCaldon, "Rape", p. 47.
15. B. Glueck, "Persons Convicted of Crimes Involving Sexual Aberrations", p. 303.
16. MacDonald, *Rape Offenders and Their Victims*, p. 66.
17. McCaldon, "Rape", p. 45.

chapter 7

1. For an elaboration of these themes, see Lorenne M.G. Clark, "The Rights of Women: The Theory and Practice of the Ideology of Male Supremacy"; Lynda Lange, "Reproduction in Democratic Theory"; and Mary O'Brien, "The Politics of Impotence", in *Contemporary Issues in Political Philosophy*, Canadian Contemporary Philosophy Series, ed. J. King-Farlow and W.R. Shea (New York: Science History Publications, 1976).
2. R.E. Megarry, *A Manual of the Law of Real Property*, 2d ed. (London: Stevens & Sons, Ltd., 1955), p. 538.
3. Ibid., p. 291: "From the Fourteenth Century to 1939 there was in general no restriction upon a testator's power to dispose of property as he thought fit: for good reasons or bad, he might give all his property to a mistress or to charities and leave his family penniless."

4. Edward Shorter, *The Making of the Modern Family* (New York: Basic Books, 1975). For a thorough discussion of the extent to which marriage before 1750 was "held together by considerations of property and lineage" rather than by ties of affection, see especially chapter 2, from which the above quotation is taken (p. 55). This point is further elaborated in chapter 4, in which it is argued that interest rather than affection was the main factor determining who married whom. The following is from p. 142: "Make no mistake: the parents of the couple *had* to approve, because to spite parental will was to risk disinheritance, and in a society where capital was inherited, not accumulated, exclusion from your patrimony automatically consigned you to a marginal existence—not to mention having to endure the anguish of community opprobrium if you started keeping house without the proper sanctification."

5. Recent Supreme Court decisions in the *Rathwell* and *Murdoch* cases make it quite clear that no matter how much a wife may contribute to family assets, she is not entitled to an equal share of such property in the event that the marriage is dissolved.

6. Shorter, *The Making of the Modern Family*. Chapter 6 outlines the methods of community control exercised in "traditional society" in order to enforce socially acceptable practices and to discourage those out of keeping with community norms. He points out, on p. 222, that "the community, sensitive to any usurpation of husbandly authority, was especially quick to strike down public manifestations of feminine strength."

7. Ibid., p. 75: "...women's work was found in sex and reproduction: sleeping with their husbands on demand and producing babies up to the limits set by community norms." According to Shorter, women were regarded as little more than baby machines, and were regarded as easily replaced (pp. 57–58 and p. 77). He remarks further, on p. 145, that "the need to marry big, strong women able to shoulder their full share of work may have blinded peasants to the delicacy of line and fineness of feature that constitute our modern ideal of feminine beauty."

8. Adelyn Bowland, "The Source and Development of Rape Law in England to 1820", unpublished. We are greatly indebted to this work for its thorough analysis of original sources and for its absolute verification of the hypothesis that rape laws were primarily intended to limit the acquisition of property rights.

9. Megarry, *A Manual of the Law of Real Property*, p. 538.

10. Shorter, *The Making of the Modern Family*. This book points out that during the Middle Ages, when our modern offence of rape first begins to emerge, the vast majority of people never formally "married" at all. "In the eyes of medieval society, a couple who plighted their troth without undergoing the formality of a legal ceremony would still be considered as married by the surrounding society, even though the offspring might be recorded as illegitimate" (p. 85.). Marriage was not fully sacramentalized until the Reformation and was, prior to that time, more a secular than a

religious rite. The further back one goes the clearer it is that the roots of marriage lay in the necessity of providing a settled method of property transfer. Thus, during the medieval period, the persons most likely to go through the formalities were precisely those who had property to worry about.

chapter 9

1. William C. Perdue and David Lester, "Personality Characteristics of Rapists", p. 514. This article reports that, on the basis of Rorshach tests administered to convicted rapists as part of parole proceedings, "rapists did not differ from the control groups in race, IQ or the total number of Rorschach responses. The rapists, were, however, significantly older than those convicted of aggressive non-sexual crimes....It is clear that these rapists did not differ significantly from the 15 men convicted of aggressive non-sexual crimes on any of the Rorschach variables. It may be concluded that, on parole from prison, rapists do not differ significantly from those convicted of aggressive non-sexual crimes."

2. See, for example, B. Karpman's study of rape. This work is an excellent illustration of the extent to which early investigators were convinced that sexual offenders in general must be grossly abnormal, and of the extent to which the actual data gathered did not support this assumption. Throughout his book, Karpman refers to sexual offenders as mentally ill and mentally abnormal, but the data he presents is always contradictory. For every study that finds evidence of gross psychopathy, two or three others fail to find it; and in the end, the most that can be said is that such persons exhibit "inadequate personalities" and "sociopathic tendencies". It hardly needs to be pointed out such terms are somewhat less than diagnostic. Given that psychiatrists are not generally inclined toward finding the people they are called upon to assess to be "normal" (particularly when these people are being assessed against their will, and have been convicted of offences which deeply offend some people's moral sensibilities), some labels have to be found for them. These were the strongest terms Karpman could come up with, but they certainly do not distinguish rapists from other sexual offenders, sexual offenders from other groups of prisoners, or—one suspects—these persons from a random sample of the male population at large. The following quotations from the text amply illustrate our point: "Long before the sex fiend reaches his eventual crime of violence he has given ample evidence of his tendencies"; and "No man can guarantee when another man will or will not commit a sex crime". *The Sexual Offender and His Offences*, pp. 274-275.

3. See notes 2 and 4 for this chapter.

4. R.J. McCladon, "Rape", p. 57. The author concludes that of the 30 convicted rapists he studied, "half of them are impulsively sociopathic, and

rape is only one of many antisocial tendencies. The other half have a specific hostility to women, and tend to be more violent, especially if their personality is schizoid. Their misogyny may have its roots in preoedipal frustrations. Their therapeutic potential is not high, but some seem to mellow with the passage of time."

P. Gebhard, J. Gagnon, W. Pomeroy and C. Christensen, in *Sex Offenders: An Analysis of Types*, conclude that clinicians responsible for the treatment of sex offenders with mental and emotional problems have estimated a low incidence of psychosis: from less than 1% to no more than 5%.

John M. MacDonald concurs with the findings of Gebhard *et al*, concluding that the "majority have some form of character disorder. Alcoholism and homosexuality are frequently encountered, but some men convicted of rape do not have any mental disorder" (*Rape Offenders and Their Victims*, p. 56). It is certainly striking that a psychiatrist will conclude that some rapists are free of any kind of mental disorder, but fail to see that the misogyny so characteristic of the rapist could properly be termed a disorder.

5. For a striking illustration of this fact, see the article on Gary Addison Taylor in "Crime", *Time*, 9 June, 1975: "Taylor has a long history of violence against women, beginning at age 18. Now, at age 39, he appears to have been responsible for the deaths of at least six women, and for the sexual abuse of at least four others. At the time of his first offence, a psychiatrist testified in court that 'he is unreasonably hostile toward women, and this makes it very possible that he might very well kill a person.' However, despite this finding, Dr. Ames Robey, the Director of the Michigan Center for Forensic Psychiatry, diagnosed Taylor's condition as a character disorder and not a treatable mental illness, and Taylor was released."

6. F. Emanuel Hammer, "A Comparison of H-T-P's of Rapists and Pedophiles", pp. 346–354.

7. G.R. Pascal and F.I. Herzberg, "The Detection of Deviant Sexual Practice from Performance on the Rorschach Test", p. 369.

8. McCaldon, "Rape", p. 37.

9. Ibid., p. 38.

10. "The Law", *Time*, 12 May, 1975.

11. The recent California trial of Inez Garcia illustrates this point all too clearly. Inez was raped by one man while another watched. Twenty minutes after the rape, having returned to her home and gone out again, she shot and killed her assailant. She was tried for murder, and evidence concerning the rape was not allowed to be introduced in her defence. The judge held such evidence to be irrelevant, since the trial was for murder and not for rape. She was convicted. The attitudes of jurors interviewed after the conclusion of the trial reveal very clearly that men believe a man's

motivation for rape is simply the desire for sexual intercourse, and that the method used to secure female co-operation is irrelevant. Only the actual infliction of physical harm is unacceptable. One of the jurors, when asked if a woman could ever argue self-defence if she killed a man during an attempted rape, replied: "No, because the guy's not trying to kill her. He's just trying to give her a good time. To get off, the guy will have to do her bodily harm, and giving a girl a screw isn't doing her bodily harm." He also added "...when I leave here, I'll have less fear of raping a woman now than I did before. At least I know that if I get shot, she won't get away." He also made it clear that when he said this, "I was thinking of all the men out there reading it." This juror clearly saw that convicting Inez Garcia for murder was tantamount to giving men a license to rape with impunity. It announced to the world that no woman has the right to defend herself against her attacker, since he does not intend to cause her physical injury. A rapist could be exonerated even if he did harm his victim, because he could always claim that he did not intend such harm, and that it came about only because of the coercive methods he had to use to make her co-operate. A full account of this case and its aftermath is given in *Ms. Magazine*, May, 1975.

12. "Crime", *Time*, 26 May, 1975. This article was a preliminary review of the problem of rape, and the status of rape research in Canada.

chapter 10

1. William Ryan, "The Art of Savage Discovery: How to Blame the Victim", *Victimology*, ed. Israel Drapkin and Emilio Viano, p. 149.
2. Ibid., p. 150.
3. What we are saying here about the application of victimology to the problem of rape is in no way meant to be a castigation of the discipline of victimology in general. The developing branch of criminology and sociology described as "victimology" has made valuable contributions to the theory and study of crime. And it is motivated by altogether laudable goals in wanting to see the perspective of the victim— whether of crime, social injustice, or natural disabilities—adequately represented in the theory and methodology of the social sciences. But like most good things, it can be badly applied, or misapplied by those of lesser ability who mistake justification for explanation.
4. Ryan, "The Art of Savage Discovery", p. 155.
5. Beniamin Mendelsohn, "The Origin of the Doctrine of Victimology", *Victimology*, p. 3.
6. Ibid., p. 4.
7. Ibid.
8. Ibid.
9. This idea, of course, is not unique to Mendelsohn. The legal system itself

institutionalizes this belief in the special regulations which have tradition-ally applied to rape cases.

10. Mendelsohn, "The Doctrine of Victimology", p. 5. Mendelsohn does not define precisely what he means by this term. Presumably, it is only a formalization of the idea that "when a woman says no, she often means yes". Again, it is essentially irrelevant what the woman means; the only thing that matters is what the offender *thinks* she means, or what he be-lieves to be acceptable behaviour under the circumstances. The sexual self-determination of the woman involved is simply not a factor in rape situations—nor, for that matter, in many situations which technically are not rape.

11. Ibid.

12. Menachem Amir, *Patterns in Forcible Rape*, p. 266.

13. Ibid.

14. Ibid., pp. 268-269. Amir claims that alcohol was present in the victim in 35.1% of the victim-precipitated cases (as compared with 17.9% of the cases which were not victim-precipitated); the victim was alleged to have a "bad reputation" in 32.9% of the victim-precipitated cases (as com-pared with 16.7%), and to have met the offender at a bar or picnic in 23.8% of these cases (compared with 7.2%).

15. Ibid., p. 266.

16. Ibid., p. 262.

17. Wolfgang supervised much of Amir's work and supplied the introduc-tion to the Philadelphia study. He does not seem to be aware, unfortunately, of the difficulties in applying a concept similar to his "victim-precipitated criminal homicide" to rape.

18. Marvin E. Wolfgang, *Patterns in Criminal Homicide*, p. 252.

19. Ibid.

20. John M. MacDonald, *Rape Offenders and Their Victims*, p. 78.

21. Ibid., p. 79.

22. Ibid.

23. Rape is a method whereby men revenge themselves against other men by destroying property which is valuable to them. For example, the follow-ing headline and partial text of an item appeared in the *Vancouver Daily Province*, 12 May, 1975, from U.P.I. (datelined Philadelphia):

> GIRLS RAPED, BURNED: REVENGE THE MOTIVE?
> The rape and gasoline fire torture of two 16-year-old girls, one of whom died, may have been revenge for a beating given the father of one of their two assailants. Police said the dead girl, and her com-panion...may have been attacked in vengeance for a severe beating given to ——, former owner of a discotheque, by a group of men two nights earlier.

chapter 11

1. A good illustration of this point is made in the following item from the *Washington Post*, reprinted in the "No Comment" section of *Ms. Magazine*, January, 1976, p. 83:

   > Richeson's defense attorney, Howard, hailed the judge's decision to sentence his client concurrently as "fair...and a smashing victory. He doesn't have to spend one extra day in jail for the rape." Howard said that as a man he was unable to place himself in the victim's shoes, but he noted the medical report showed only bruises. "It's not the kind of aggravated case of a young girl who is going to be permanently scarred," he said.

   As long as rape is treated as a purely sexual offence, the way will be open to showing that the victim was *lucky* for this unexpected opportunity to have sexual intercourse. This perspective simply refuses to acknowledge that the circumstances of the act radically alters its character. This tradition of treating rape merely as a form of sexual intercourse in amply illustrated by the remainder of the *Washington Post* item:

   > The attorney had one other thought. "Here was a 47-year-old woman with three children who—to put it in a crude way—she might be glad to have it happen...."

   However, this particular species of gross insult to women is even better illustrated from a source at home. An article entitled, "Making Your One Phone Call Count", which appeared in *The Canadian Magazine*, 19 July, 1975, chronicles the exploits of Canada's top ten criminal defence lawyers. The following story is told about one such legal luminary:

   > A Crown Attorney recalls what he thought was an open-and-shut case against _____'s client caught by a cop in the very act of trying to rape a blind woman. "Who could *lose* such a case?" asked the Crown. "Then _____ started with his cross-examination. He didn't get nasty with the woman or anything. But she was a little creepy and not too good looking and by the time he was finished, he made it seem his client was almost doing this woman a favour because it was the only chance she'd ever get to...you know what I mean? I could see what he was doing and knew that I'd lost."

   To hold this up as an example of brilliant legal strategy hardly says anything very admirable about the concept of justice alleged to underlie our criminal justice system. But it makes as clear as anything could that so long as rape is regarded as a purely sexual offence, no woman, not even those who are blind or otherwise in need of more rather than less protection, can be safely assured protection from potential risks to their lives, as well as to their autonomy.

2. Ann Wolbert Burgess and Lynda Lytle Holmstrom, "Rape Trauma Syndrome", pp. 981-986. In reporting on the immediate and long-term effects of rape on women, the authors describe the effect as a "rape trauma

syndrome" which they define as follows:

"The rape trauma syndrome, consisting of behavioural, somatic, and psychological reactions in the acute phase and a long-term reorganization process, is an acute stress reaction to a *life-threatening situation*" (emphasis ours).

They note further that the prominent feeling experienced by the victim is fear, and that the physical symptoms of the victim are those characteristic of this feeling.

recommendations

1. Lorenne M.G. Clark and Debra J. Lewis, "A Study of Rape in Canada: Phases C and D".
2. Lorenne M.G. Clark and Simon Armstrong, "A Review of Past, Present and Projected Rape Research".
3. R.J. McCaldon, "Rape", p. 57.
4. Clark and Armstrong, "A Review of Past, Present and Projected Rape Research". This work catalogues present and projected rape research in Canada. Since this report is at the moment confidential, it is not possible to describe in detail the nature of this research. However, several major projects centre around the offender and on new treatment methods, though all of these would seem to be cast within the framework of established psychiatric classification.

bibliography

Amir, Menachem. *Patterns in Forcible Rape*. Chicago: University of Chicago Press, 1971.

——————————. "Victim Precipitated Forcible Rape." *The Journal of Criminal Law, Criminology and Police Science* 58 (1967).

Brownmiller, Susan. *Against Our Will: Men, Women and Rape*. New York: Simon & Schuster, 1975.

Burgess, Ann Wolbert; and Holmstrom, Lynda Lytle. "Rape Trauma Syndrome." *American Journal of Psychiatry* 121, no. 9 (1974).

Canada. Bureau of Statistics. *Crime Statistics (Police)*, 1961, 1962 and 1971. Ottawa: Queen's Printer.

Chappell, Duncan; Geis, Gilbert; and Fogarty, Faith. "Forcible Rape: Bibliography." *Journal of Criminal Law and Criminology* 65, no. 2 (1974).

Chappell, Duncan; Geis, Gilbert; Schafer, Stephen; and Siegel, Larry. "Forcible Rape: A Comparative Study of Offenses Known to the Police in Boston and Los Angeles." *Studies in the Sociology of Sex*, edited by James M. Henslin. New York: Appleton, Century, Crofts, 1971.

Chappell, Duncan; and Singer, Susan. "Rape in New York City: A Study of Material in the Police Files and Its Meaning." Unpublished manuscript, 1973.

Chesler, Phyllis. *Women and Madness*. New York: Garden City Press, 1972.

Clark, Lorenne M.G. "Politics and Law: The Theory and Practice of the Ideology of Male Supremacy." *Contemporary Issues in Political Philosophy*. Edited by J. King-Farlow and W. Shea. New York: Science History Publications, 1976.

——————————. "Rape in Toronto: Psychosocial Perspectives on the Offender." *Human Sexuality in Canada: A Source Book*. Edited by B. Schlesinger. Toronto: University of Toronto Press, forthcoming.

Clark, Lorenne M.G.; and Armstrong, Simon. "A Study of Rape in Canada: A Review of Past, Present and Projected Rape Research." *Report to the Solicitor-General of Canada, 1975*. Monograph. Canada: Ministry of the Solicitor-General, forthcoming.

Clark, Lorenne M.G.; Barr-Carley, Margaret; and Ward, Mary. "A Study of Rape in Canada: Phases A and B." *Report to the National Law Reform Commission of Canada, 1975*.

Connell, Noreen; and Wilson, Cassandra, eds. *Rape: The First Source Book for Women*. New York: New American Library, 1974.

Dixon, G. "Corroboration of the Complainant's Testimony in a Sexual Offense." *Alberta Law Review*, 1969.

Drapkin, Israel; and Viano, Emilio, eds. *Victimology*. Lexington, Mass.: D.C. Heath & Co., 1974.

Gebhard, P.; Gagnon, J.; Pomeroy, W.; and Christenson, C. *Sex Offenders: An Analysis of Types*. New York: Harper & Row, 1965.

Giffen, P.J. "Rates of Crime and Delinquency." *Crime and Its Treatment in Canada*. Edited by W.T. McGrath. Toronto: Macmillan of Canada, 1965.

Gigeroff, A.; and Mohr, J.W. "A Study of Male Sexual Offenders." *Canada's Mental Health* 13, no. 3 (1965).

Glueck, B. "Final Report, Research Project for the Study and Treatment of Persons Convicted of Crimes Involving Sexual Aberrations." June 1952-June 1955.

Griffin, Susan. "Rape: The All-American Crime." *Ramparts Magazine* 10 (1971).

Hammer, Emanuel, F. "A Comparison of H-T-P's of Rapists and Pedophiles." *Journal of Projective Techniques* 18 (1954).

Hibey, R.A. "The Trial of a Rape Case: An Advocate's Analysis of Corroboration, Consent and Character." *American Criminal Law Review* 11, no. 2 (1973).

Hood, Roger; and Sparks, Richard. *Key Issues in Criminology*. New York: McGraw-Hill, 1971.

Karpman, B. *The Sexual Offender and His Offenses: Etiology, Pathology, Psychodynamics, and Treatment*. New York: Julian Press, 1954.

Lange, Lynda. "Reproduction in Democratic Theory." *Contemporary Issues in Political Philosophy*. Edited by J. King-Farlow and W. Shea. New York: Science History Publications, 1976.

Lewis, Debra J. "Rape in Toronto: An Analysis of Rape Complaints Received by the Metropolitan Toronto Police Department in 1970. " M.A. Thesis, University of Toronto, 1974.

McCaldon, R.J. "Rape." *Canadian Journal of Corrections* 9, no. 37 (1967).

MacDonald, John M. *Rape Offenders and Their Victims*. Springfield: Charles C. Thomas, 1971.

McDonald, William F. *The Victim: A Social Psychological Study of Criminal Victimization*. Ph.D. Thesis, University of California, 1970.

Margolin, D. "Rape: The Facts." *Women: A Journal of Liberation* 3, no. 1 (1973).

Medea, Andra; and Thompson, Kathleen. *Against Rape: A Survival Manual for Women*. New York: Farrar, Straus & Giroux, 1974.

Megarry, R.E. *A Manual of the Law of Real Property*. 2d ed. London: Stevens, 1955.

Mendelsohn, Beniamin. "The Origin of the Doctrine of Victimology". *Victimology*. Edited by Israel Drapkin and Emilio Viano. Lexington, Mass.: D.C. Heath & Co., 1974.

Mohr, J.W. "Sexual Behaviour and the Criminal Law, Part III. Rape and Attempted Rape." Preliminary Report, Forensic Clinic. Toronto: Toronto Psychiatric Hospital, 1965.

O'Brien, Mary. "The Politics of Impotence." *Contemporary Issues in Political Philosophy*. Edited by J. King-Farlow and W. Shea. New York: Science History Publications, 1976.

Pascal, G.R.; and Herzberg, F.I. "The Detection of Deviant Sexual Practice from Performance on the Rorschach Test." *Journal of Projective Techniques* 16 (1952).

Perdue, William C.; and Lester, David. "Personality Characteristics of Rapists." *Perceptual and Motor Skills* 35 (1972).

Radzinowicz, L.; and the Cambridge Department of Criminal Sciences. *Sexual Offenses*. London: Macmillan & Co., 1957.

Ringrose, C.A. Douglas. "Sociological, Medical and Legal Aspects of Rape." *Criminal Law Quarterly* 17, no. 4 (1975).

Russell, Diana. *The Politics of Rape: The Victim's Perspective*. New York: Stein & Day, 1975.

Ryan, William. "The Art of Savage Discovery: How to Blame the Victim." *Victimology*. Edited by Israel Drapkin and Emilio Viano. Lexington, Mass.: D.C. Heath & Co., 1974.

Schafer, Stephen. *The Criminal and His Victim*. New York: Random House, 1968.

Schultz, G.D. *How Many More Victims?* Philadelphia: J.B. Lippincott, 1965.

Svalastoga, K. "Rape and Social Structure." *Pacific Sociological Review* 5, no. 48 (1962).

U.S. *Presidential Commission on Law Enforcement and the Administration of Justice*. 1967.

Von Hentig, Hans. *The Criminal and His Victim*. New Haven: Yale University Press, 1948.

Wolfgang, Marvin E. *Patterns in Criminal Homicide*. Philadelphia: University of Pennsylvania Press, 1958.

Wood, Pamela Lakes. "The Victim in a Forcible Rape Case: A Feminist View." *American Criminal Law Review* 11:2 (1973).